USE YOUR

HEAD

TONY BUZAN

BRITISH BROADCASTING CORPORATION

Other books by Tony Buzan

Speed Memory
Speed Reading
Spore One
Advanced Learning and Reading – Manual
    (with Bernard Chibnall)
The Evolving Brain
Make the most of your mind

Acknowledgement is due to the University of Technology,
Loughborough for two photographs and information for the
diagram on holography, page 99.

The diagrams, both colour and black-and-white, are by
Brian Mayers Associates with the exception of the drawings of
the brain and eye by Mary Waldron (pages 12 and 27), and
the drawings on pages 14 and 15 by Robinson Farrens.

A series of ten television programmes *Use your head*
produced by Nancy Thomas.
First broadcast on BBC 2 from January 1974.

Published to accompany a series of programmes
prepared in consultation with the
BBC Further Education Advisory Council

First published 1974 Reprinted 1974 (three times), 1975, 1976 (three times), 1977,
1978, 1979, 1980 (two times)

Published by the British Broadcasting Corporation
35 Marylebone High Street, London W1M 4AA
Printed in England by
Jolly & Barber Ltd., Rugby

ISBN 0 563 10790 1

dedicated
to
YOU

With thanks to all those whose effort and co-operation
enabled me to write this book:

Zita Albes; Astrid Andersen; Jeannie Beattie;
Nick Beytes; Mark Brown; Joy Buttery;
Bernard Chibnall; Steve and Fanny Colling;
Susan Crockford; Lorraine Gill;
Bill Harris; Brian Helweg-Larsen;
Thomas Jarlov; Trish Lillis; Hermione Lovell;
Annette McGee; Joe McMahon;
My Parents and Brother; Khalid Ranjah;
Auriol Roberts; Ian Rosenbloom;
Caitrina Ni Shuilleabhain;
Robert Millard Smith; Chris and Pat Stevens;
Jan Streit; Christopher Tatham;
Lee Taylor; Nancy Thomas;
Jim Ward; Bill Watts; Gillian Watts.

Contents

The patterns on the following pages represent a new method for noting.

There are eight of them, and they summarise the chapters of the book.

In these 'brain patterns' key words are linked to each other around a main centre (in these cases, the overall theme of a chapter), and a mental picture is built up of an entire thought structure.

- Before starting to read the book, take a quick look at the chapters (commencing page 83) where the theory and method for making these patterned notes is fully outlined.

- Use the notes for each chapter as a preview of what is to come; they will make the reading of the chapter easier.

- After finishing a chapter, look at its patterns once again. This will serve as a good review, and will help you to remember what you have read.

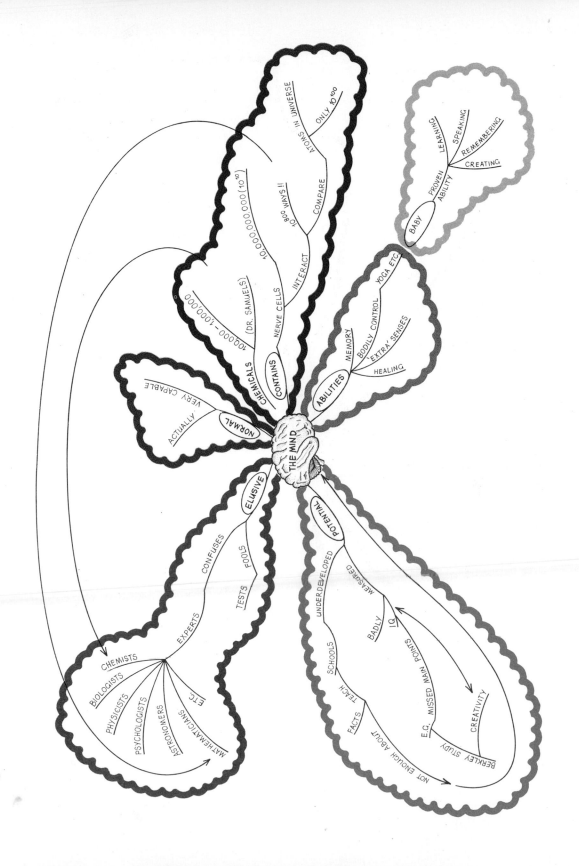

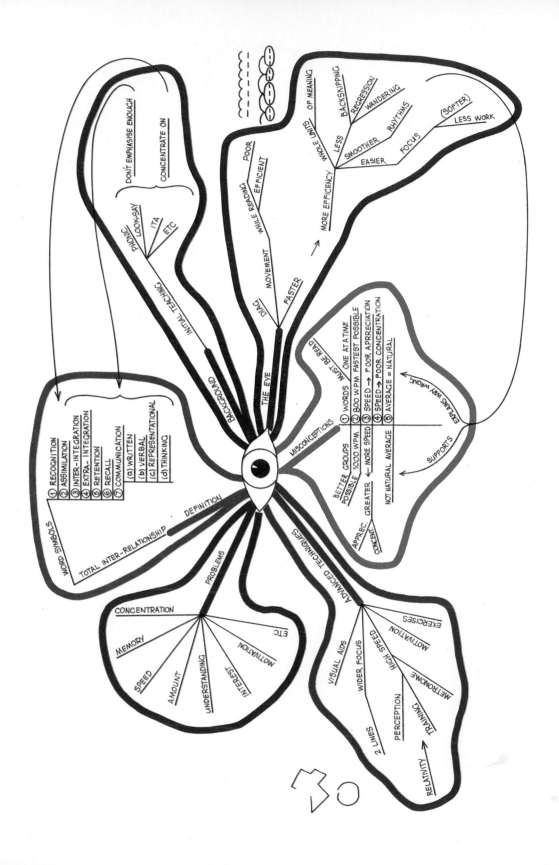

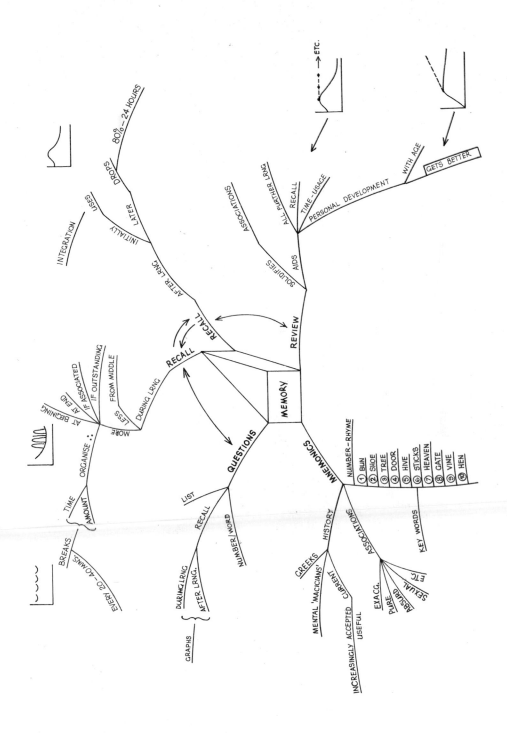

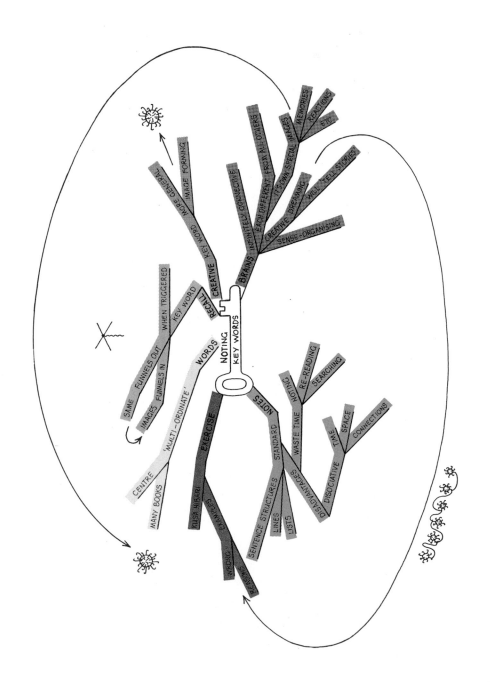

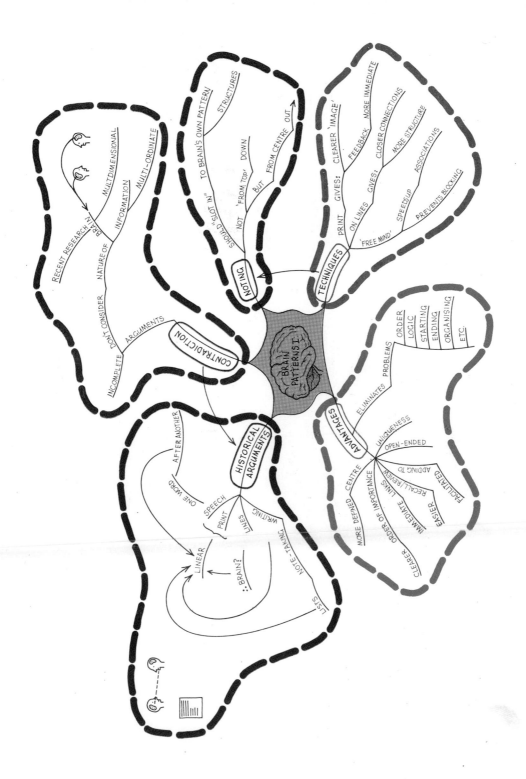

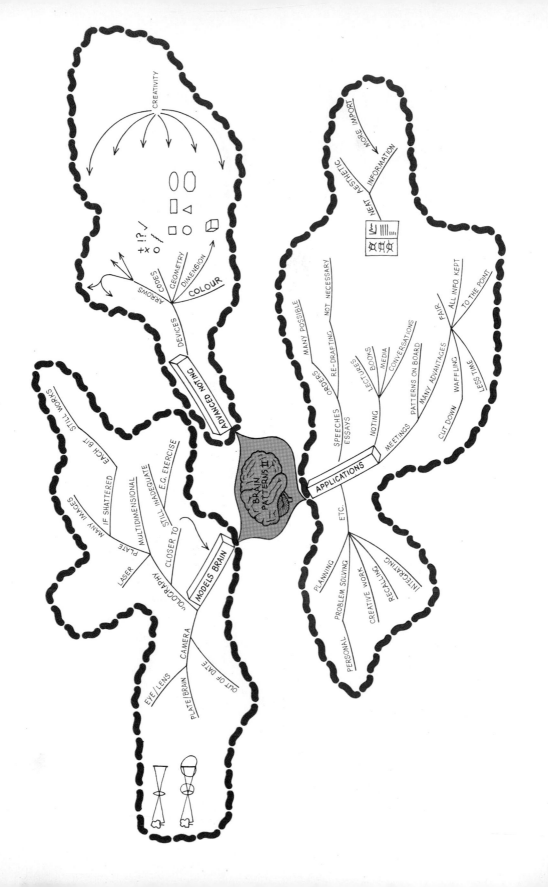

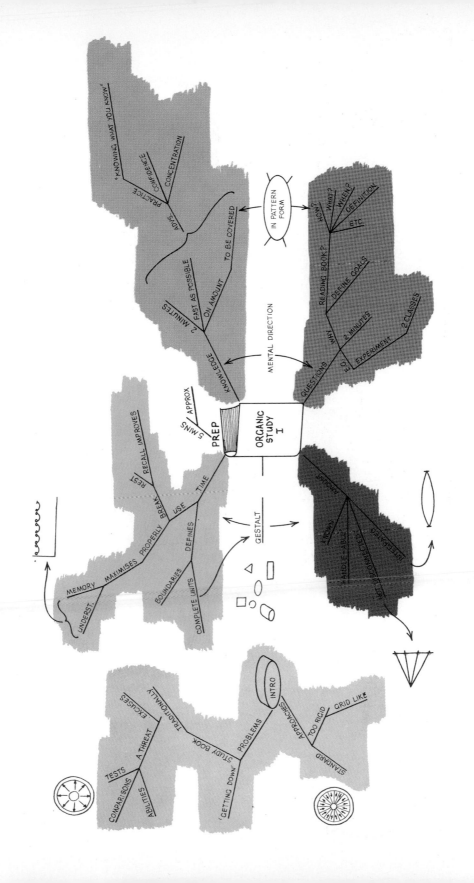

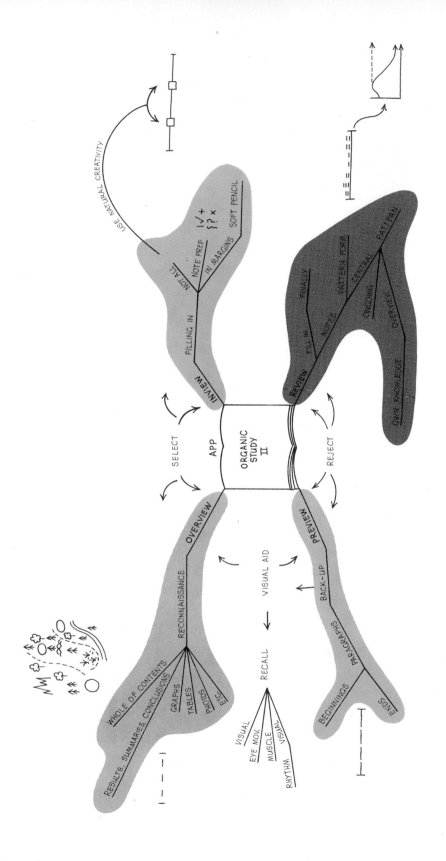

You and this book

Use your head is written to help you do just that. By the time you have finished the book you should be able to study more effectively, solve problems more readily, read faster and more efficiently, and know generally much more about how your mind works and how to use it to the best advantage.

This introductory section gives general guide lines about the book's contents, and the ways in which these contents are best approached.

The chapters

Each chapter deals with a different aspect of your brain's functioning. First the book applies current information about the brain to the way in which our vision can be best used.

Next, a chapter explains how you can improve memory both after and during learning. In addition a special system is introduced for perfectly memorising listed items.

The middle chapters explore the brain's internal patterns. This information about how we think is applied to the way in which we use language and words for recording, organising, remembering, creative thinking and problem solving.

The last chapters deal with the Organic Study Method. Rather than being one of the simple grid methods such as the SQ3R, the Organic Study Method will enable you to study any subject ranging from English to Higher Mathematics.

Your effort

It is essential that you practise if you wish to be able to use effectively the methods and information outlined. At various stages in the book there are exercises and suggestions for further activity. In addition you should work out your own practice and study schedule, keeping to it as firmly as possible.

Personal notes

At the end of each chapter you will find pages for 'Personal Notes'. These are for any odd jottings you might wish to make during reading and can also be used when you discover relevant information after you have 'finished' the book.

The Personal Notes should also prove useful in connection with the television series *Use your head*. The chapter headings and television programmes are not identical but the information in each supports and adds to the other. Much information from the programmes could be usefully recorded in your Personal Notes.

The principle underlying these pages is that *Use your head,* being an informational book, is not simply a record of the author's personal views, but also allows the reader to criticise, comment, record and supplement the information.
For this reason the book has been planned with wide margins, in which you are encouraged to add your own thoughts.

Bibliography

On page 143 you will find a special list of books. These are not just books of academic reference, but include books which will help you develop your general knowledge as well as giving you more specialised information concerning some of the areas covered in *Use your head*.

The Time-Life books give clear and graphic accounts of such topics as Vision and the Mind, and can be used most effectively for family reading and study.

My own book, *Speed memory*, is a combination of the special memory techniques for recalling lists, numbers, names and faces, etc. It should be used in conjunction with the information from the Memory chapter.

You and yourself

It is hoped that *Use your head* will help you to expand as an individual, and that through an increasing awareness of yourself you will be able to develop your own ways of thinking.

Each person using information from this book starts with different levels of learning ability, and will progress at the pace best suited to him. It is important therefore to measure improvement in relation to yourself and not others.

Although much of the information has been presented in connection with reading, formal noting and studying, the complete application is much wider. When you have finished and reviewed the book, browse through it again to see in which other areas of your life the information can be helpfully applied.

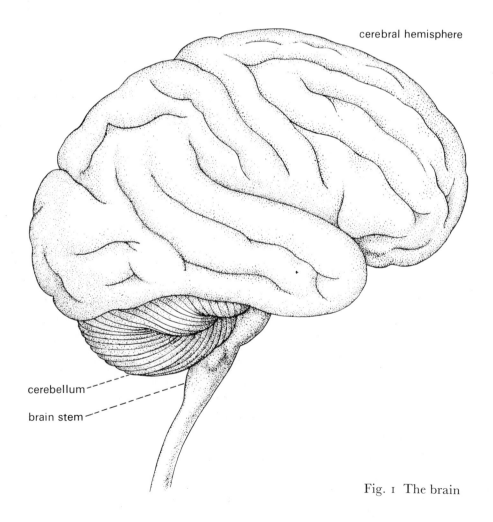

cerebral hemisphere

cerebellum

brain stem

Fig. 1 The brain

Your mind is better than you think

It is only in the last 150 years that any real progress has been made in man's understanding of his own mind, and even that progress has shown us little in comparison to what there is to be known. At the moment, despite the fact that we know the various parts of the brain, know much about the way in which chemicals change inside it, know about DNA and RNA, and know about certain experimental results under restricted conditions, we are still struggling with what must be the most elusive quarry man has ever chased.

Just when we think we have located areas where activities such as thinking, remembering and speaking are based, up pops a situation which proves that the answer is by no means certain; and just when tests seem to prove that the mind works in a given way, along comes another test which proves that it doesn't work that way at all, or along comes another human being with a brain which manages to make the test meaningless.

What we *are* gathering from our efforts at the moment is a knowledge that the mind is infinitely more subtle than we previously thought, and that everyone who has what is ironically called a 'normal' mind has a much larger ability and potential than was previously thought.

A few examples will help to make this clear.

13

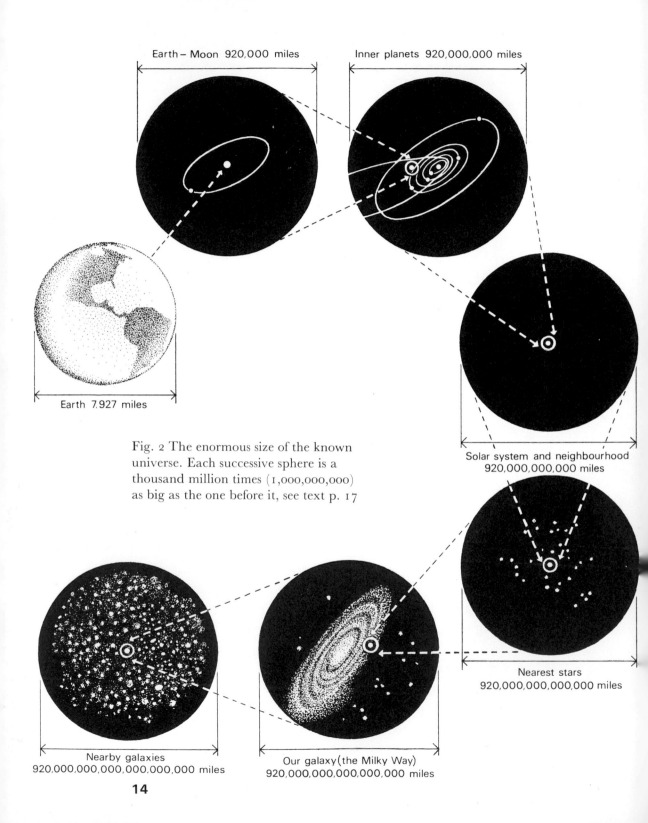

Earth – Moon 920,000 miles

Inner planets 920,000,000 miles

Earth 7.927 miles

Fig. 2 The enormous size of the known universe. Each successive sphere is a thousand million times (1,000,000,000) as big as the one before it, see text p. 17

Solar system and neighbourhood
920,000,000,000 miles

Nearest stars
920,000,000,000,000 miles

Nearby galaxies
920,000,000,000,000,000,000 miles

Our galaxy (the Milky Way)
920,000,000,000,000,000 miles

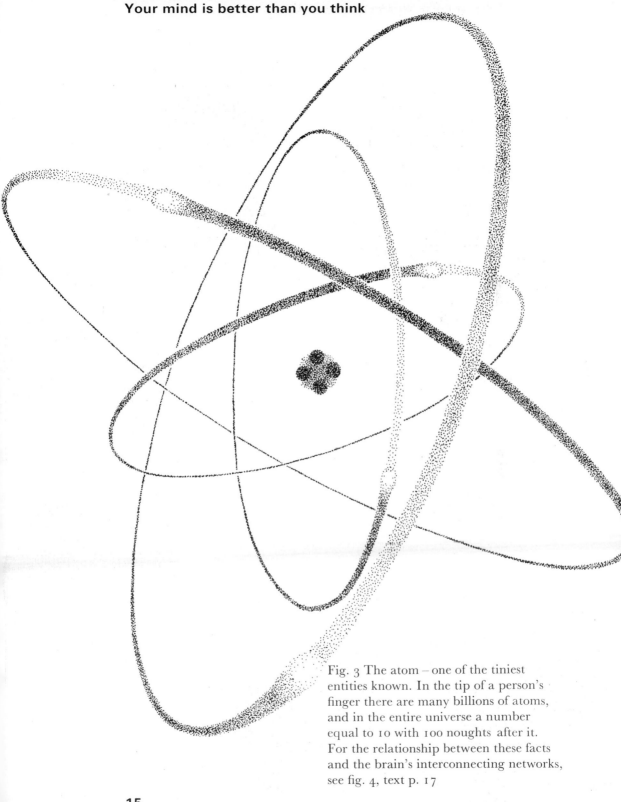

Fig. 3 The atom – one of the tiniest
entities known. In the tip of a person's
finger there are many billions of atoms,
and in the entire universe a number
equal to 10 with 100 noughts after it.
For the relationship between these facts
and the brain's interconnecting networks,
see fig. 4, text p. 17

10,000,000,000,000,000,000,000,000,000,000,000,
000,000,000,000,000,000,000,000,000,000,000,000
000,000,000,000,000,000,000

Fig. 4a The number of atoms (one of the smallest particles we know of) in the known universe (the largest thing we know of). See text p. 17.

10,000,000,000,000,000,000,000,000,000,000,000,
000,000,000,000,000,000,000,000,000,000,000,000,
000,000,000,000,000,000,000,000,000,000,000,000,
000,000,000,000,000,000,000,000,000,000,000,000,
000,000,000,000,000,000,000,000,000,000,000,000,
000,000,000,000,000,000,000,000,000,000,000,000,
000,000,000,000,000,000,000,000,000,000,000,000,
000,000,000,000,000,000,000,000,000,000,000,000,
000,000,000,000,000,000,000,000,000,000,000,000,
000,000,000,000,000,000,000,000,000,000,000,000,
000,000,000,000,000,000,000,000,000,000,000,000,
000,000,000,000,000,000,000,000,000,000,000,000,
000,000,000,000,000,000,000,000,000,000,000,000,
000,000,000,000,000,000,000,000,000,000,000,000,
000,000,000,000,000,000,000,000,000,000,000,000,
000,000,000,000,000,000,000,000,000,000,000,000,
000,000,000,000,000,000,000,000,000,000,000,000,
000,000,000,000,000,000,000,000,000,000,000,000,
000,000,000,000,000,000,000,000,000,000,000,000,
000,000

Fig. 4b The number of estimated interconnections and patterns the 10,000,000,000, individual neurons of one brain can make. See text p. 17.

Most of the more scientific disciplines, despite their apparent differences of direction, are all being drawn into a whirlpool, the centre of which is the mind. Chemists are now involved with the intricate chemical structures that exist and interact inside our heads; biologists are struggling with the brain's biological functions; physicists are finding parallels with their investigations into the farthest reaches of space; psychologists are trying to pin the mind down and are finding the experience frustratingly like trying to place a finger on a little globule of mercury; and mathematicians who have constructed models for complex computers and even for the Universe itself, still can't come up with a formula for the operations that go on regularly inside each of our heads every day of our lives.

Dr David Samuels of the Weizmann Institute recently estimated that in one average brain there are between 100,000 to 1,000,000 different chemicals reacting.

We also know that in an average brain there are 10,000,000,000 individual neurons or nerve cells. This figure becomes even more astounding when it is realised that each neuron can interact with other neurons in not just one, but many ways – it has been recently estimated that the number of interconnections may be as many as 10 with eight hundred noughts following it. To realise just how enormous this number is, compare it with a mathematical fact about the Universe: one of the smallest items in the Universe is the atom. The biggest thing we know is the Universe itself. The number of atoms in the Universe is predictably enormous: 10 with one hundred noughts after it. The number of interconnections in *one* brain makes even this number seem tiny. (See figs. 2, 3 and 4).

Other examples of the mind's abilities abound – examples of extraordinary memory feats, feats of super-strength, and unusual control of body functions defying the 'laws of science', are becoming more widespread. They are now fortunately more documented, generally recognised and usefully applied.

Even with this mounting evidence a number of people still remain sceptical, pointing to the performance of most of us, suggesting that we hardly fit the description! In response to this objection a questionnaire was given to people from all areas of life. The questions are noted below, and underneath each question is noted the reply given by at least 95 per cent. As you read ask yourself the questions.

- In school were you taught anything about how your memory functions?
  No.
- Were you taught anything about special and advanced memory techniques?
  No.
- Anything about how your eye functions when you are learning, and about how you can use this knowledge to your advantage?
  No.
- Anything about the ranges of study techniques and how they can be applied to different disciplines?
  No.
- Anything about the nature of concentration and how to maintain it when necessary?
  No.
- Anything about motivation, how it effects your abilities, and how you can use it to your advantage?
  No.
- Anything about the nature of key words and key concepts and how they relate to note taking and imagination etc?
  No.
- Anything about thinking?
  No.
- Anything about creativity?
  No.

By now the answer to the original objection should be clear: the reasons why our performances do not match even our minimum potentials is that we are given no information about what we are, or about how we can best utilise our inherent capacities.

A similar reply can be given to those who say that I.Q. tests measure our 'absolute intelligence', so therefore *they* must be right.

Apart from the fact that an I. Q. score can be significantly changed by even a small amount of well directed practice, there are other arguments against these tests:

First the Berkeley Study on Creativity showed that a person whose I. Q. assessment was high was not necessarily independent in thought; independent in action; either possessed of or able to value a good sense of humour; appreciative of beauty; reasonable; relativistic; able to enjoy complexity and novelty; original; comprehensively knowledgeable; fluent; flexible; or astute. Not much is left . . . .

Secondly those who argue that I.Q. does measure a wide and absolute range of human abilities are, to use the familiar expression, not able to see the wood for the trees. The test should be concerned with three major areas: 1. the brain being tested; 2. the test itself; 3. the results. Unfortunately the I.Q. protagonists have become too obsessed with numbers 2 and 3 and have left out number 1.

They have failed to realise that their tests do not test basic human ability, but measure untrained and undeveloped human performance. Their claims are much like those of an imaginary surveyor of women's feet sizes in the Orient at the time when their feet were restricted to make them small. From the crib the foot was placed in bandages until the woman was nearly full grown. This was done to stunt the growth and to produce 'dainty' feet.

To assume, however, as the surveyor might have done, that these measurements represent natural and fully developed bodily dimensions is as absurd as it is to assume that intelligence tests measure the natural dimensions of our minds. Our minds, like the women's feet, have been 'bound' by the way we have misjudged and mistrained them, and are therefore not naturally developed.

Another and perhaps the most convincing case for the excellence of the human brain, is the human baby. Far from being the 'helpless and incapable little thing' that many people assume it to be, it is the most extraordinary learning, remembering and intellectually advanced being – even in its most early stages it surpasses the performance of the most sophisticated computers.

With very few exceptions, all babies learn to speak by the time they are two, and many even earlier. Because this is so universal it is taken for granted, but if the process is examined more closely it is seen to be extremely complex.

Try listening to someone speaking while pretending that you have no knowledge of language and very little knowledge of the objects and ideas the language discusses. Not only will this task be difficult, but because of the way sounds run into each other the distinction between different words will often be totally unclear. Every baby who has learned to talk has overcome not only these difficulties but also the difficulties of sorting out what makes sense and what doesn't. When he is confronted with sounds like 'koooochiekooochiekoooooooo-aahhhhisn'tealovelelyli'ldarling!' one wonders how he ever manages to make sense of us at all!

The young child's ability to learn language involves him in processes which include a subtle control of and an inherent understanding of rhythm, mathematics, music, physics, linguistics, spatial relations, memory, integration, creativity, logical reasoning and thinking, etc.

The reader who still doubts his own abilities has himself learned to talk and to read. He should therefore find it difficult to attack a position of which he himself is evidence for the defence!

There really is no doubt that the mind is far more capable than has been thought. The remainder of this book will attempt to shed light on a number of the areas in which performance and self-realisation can be achieved.

Personal Notes

Reading – more efficiently and faster

Overview

- Reading and learning problems
- Reading and learning – definition – the process
- Misconceptions about reading and speed reading; why they arose
- The eye
- Perception during reading and learning
- Exercises for improving comprehension and speed

Reading and learning problems

- In the space below note *all* the problems you have with reading and learning. Be strict with yourself. The more you are able to define, the more completely you will be able to improve.

- Note your own definition of the word *Reading*.

Teachers of reading and learning have noted over the past five years that in each of their classes, the same general problems arise. Below is the list of those most commonly experienced. The reader is advised to check his own against these, adding to his own list any others that apply – there will probably be quite a few.

TABLE 1 Areas in which reading and learning problems are commonly experienced.

vision	noting	recall
speed	retention	impatience
comprehension	age	vocabulary
time	fear	subvocalisation
amount	fatigue	typographic style
surroundings	laziness	literary style
	boredom	selection
	interest	rejection
	analysis	concentration
	criticism	back-skipping
	motivation	
	appreciation	
	organisation	
	regression	

Each of the problems in the table above is serious, and can by itself disrupt reading and learning. This book is devoted to solving these problems, the current chapter being concerned primarily with vision, speed, comprehension, time and amount, and the learning environment.

Before getting down to the more physical aspects of reading I shall first define the term properly, and in the light of this definition shall explain why the wide range of problems that exist is so universally experienced.

Reading defined

Reading, which is often defined as 'getting from the book what the author intended' or 'assimilating the written word' deserves a far more complete definition. It can be defined as follows:

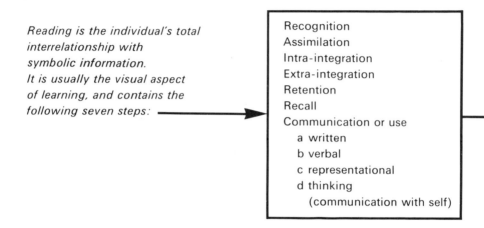

Reading is the individual's total interrelationship with symbolic information. It is usually the visual aspect of learning, and contains the following seven steps:

Recognition
Assimilation
Intra-integration
Extra-integration
Retention
Recall
Communication or use
   a written
   b verbal
   c representational
   d thinking
     (communication with self)

The definition includes consideration of most of the problems in table 1, page 23. The only problems not included are those which are, in a sense, 'outside' the reading process, 'surroundings', 'age', etc.

Why the problems exist

The reader may justifiably ask at this point why so many people experience the problems noted.

The answer lies in our approach to the initial teaching of reading. (Most of you reading this book who are over twenty-five will probably have been taught by the Phonic or Alphabet Method. Others will probably have been taught by either this or by the Look and Say Method.)

The most simplified Phonic Method teaches the child first the alphabet, then the different sounds for each of the letters

recognition

The reader's knowledge of the alphabetic symbols. This step takes place almost before the physical aspect of reading begins.

assimilation

The physical process by which light is reflected from the word and is received by the eye, then transmitted to the brain. (See fig. 5).

intra-integration

The equivalent to basic understanding, and refers to the linking of all parts of the information being read with all other appropriate parts.

extra-integration

This includes analysis, criticism, appreciation, selection and rejection. The process in which the reader brings the whole body of his previous knowledge to the new knowledge he is reading, making the appropriate connections.

retention

The basic storage of information. Storage can itself become a problem. Most readers will have experienced entering an examination room and storing most of their information during the two hour exam period! Storage, then, is not enough in itself, and must be accompanied by recall.

recall

The ability to get back out of storage that which is needed, preferably *when* it is needed.

communication

The use to which the information is immediately or eventually put; includes the very important subdivision: thinking.

in the alphabet, then the blending of sounds in syllables, and finally the blending of sounds forming words. From this point on he is given progressively difficult books, usually in the form of series graded 1 to 10, through which he progresses at his own speed. He becomes a 'silent' reader during the process.

The Look and Say Methods teach the child by presenting him with cards on which there are pictures. The names of the objects shown are clearly printed underneath them. Once a child has become familiar with the pictures and the names associated with them, the pictures are removed leaving only the words. When the child has built up enough basic vocabulary he progresses through a series of graded books similar to those for the child taught by the Phonic Method, and also becomes a 'silent' reader.

The outlines given of the two methods are necessarily brief, and there are at least fifty other methods similar to these presently being taught in England and in other English-speaking countries.

The point about these methods, however, is not that they are inadequate for achieving their aim, but that they are inadequate for teaching any child to read in the complete sense of the word.

Referring to the definition of Reading, it can be seen that these methods are designed to cover only the stage of recognition in the process, with some attempt at assimilation and intra-integration. The methods do not touch on the problems of speed, time, amount, retention, recall, selection, rejection, note-taking, concentration, appreciation, criticism, analyses, organisation, motivation, interest, boredom, surroundings, fatigue or typographic style, etc.

It can thus be seen that there is justification for the problems so widely experienced.

Recognition, it is important to note, is hardly ever mentioned as a problem, because it has been taught adequately in the early years of school. All the other problems are mentioned because they have *not* been dealt with during the educational process.

Later chapters deal with the majority of these problems. The remainder of this chapter is devoted to eye movement, comprehension and the speed of reading.

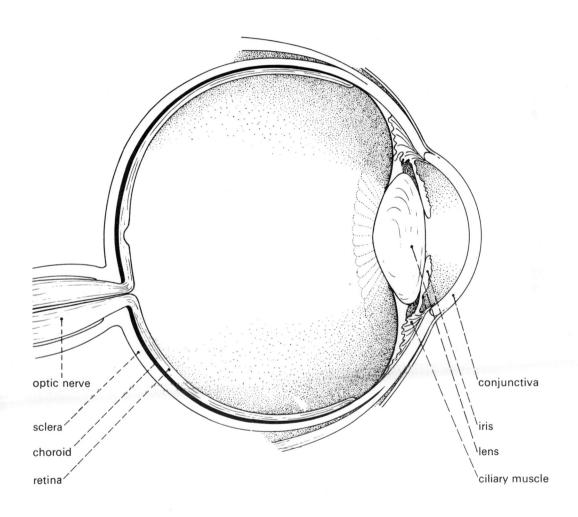

optic nerve

sclera

choroid

retina

conjunctiva

iris

lens

ciliary muscle

Fig. 5 Your eye.

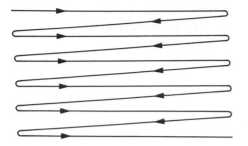

Fig. 6 Assumed reading eye movement as shown by people with no knowledge of eye movements. Each line is thought to be covered in less than one second. See text this page.

Reading eye movements

When asked to show with their fore-finger the movement and speed of their eyes as they read, most people move their fingers along in smooth lines from left to right, with a quick jump from the end of one line back to the beginning of the next. They normally take between a quarter to one second for each line. (See fig. 6).

Two major errors are being made: the movement and the speed.

Even if the eye moved as slowly as one line per second, words would be covered at the rate of 600–700 words per minute (w.p.m.). As the average reading speed on even light material is 250 w.p.m., it can be seen that even those estimating slower speeds assume that they cover words much more rapidly than they really do.

If eyes moved over print in the smooth manner shown in fig. 6 they would be able to take in nothing, because the eye can see things clearly only when it can 'hold them still'. If an object is still the eye must be still in order to see it, and if an object is moving the eye must move with the object in order to see it. A simple experiment either by yourself or with a friend will confirm this. Hold a forefinger motionless in front of the eyes and either feel your own eyes or watch your friend's eyes as they look at the object. They will remain still. Next move the finger up, down, sideways and around, following it with the eyes. And finally move the finger up, down and around, holding the eyes still, or cross both hands in front of your face, at the same time looking at them both simultane-ously. (If you can accomplish this last feat write to me immediately!) When objects move, eyes move with them if they are to be seen clearly.

Relating all this to reading, it is obvious that if the eyes are going to take in words, and if the words are still, the eyes will have to pause on each word before moving on. Rather than moving in smooth lines as shown in fig. 6, the eyes in fact move in a series of stops and quick jumps. (See fig. 7).

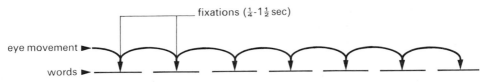

fixations ($\frac{1}{4}$-1$\frac{1}{2}$ sec)

eye movement ►

words ►

Fig. 7 Diagram representing the stop-and-start movement of the eyes during the reading process. See text this page.

The jumps themselves are so quick as to take almost no time, but the fixations can take anywhere from $\frac{1}{4}$ to 1$\frac{1}{2}$ seconds. A person who normally reads one word at a time – and who skips back over words and letters is forced, by the simple mathematics of his eye movements, into reading speeds which are often well below 100 w.p.m., and which mean that he will not be able to understand much of what he reads, nor be able to read much. (See fig. 8)

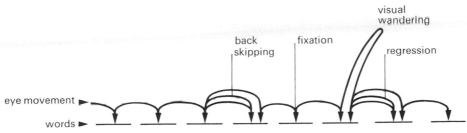

visual wandering

back skipping

fixation

regression

eye movement ►

words ►

Fig. 8 Diagram showing poor reading habits of slow reader: one word read at a time, with unconscious back-skipping, visual wandering, and conscious regressions. See text this page.

It might seem at first glance that the slow reader is doomed, but the problem can be solved, and in more than one way:

1 Skipping back over words can be eliminated, as 90 per cent of back-skipping and regression is based on apprehension and is unnecessary for understanding. The 10 per cent of words that do need to be reconsidered can be noted as explained in the chapter on Organic Study, pages 137/8.

2 The time for each fixation can be reduced to approach the $\frac{1}{4}$ second minimum – the reader need not fear that this is too short a time, for his eye is able to register as many as five words in one one-hundredth of a second.

3 The size of the fixation can be expanded to take in as many as three to five words at a time. (See fig. 9)

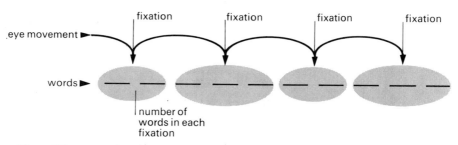

Fig. 9 Diagram showing eye movements of a better and more efficient reader. More words are taken in at each fixation, and back-skipping, regression and visual wandering are eliminated. See text this page.

This solution might at first seem impossible if it is true that the mind deals with one word at a time. In fact it can equally well fixate on *groups* of words, which is better in nearly all ways: When we read a sentence we do not read it for the individual meaning of each word, but for the meaning of the phrases in which the words are contained.

Reading for example, 'the   cat
                sat   on   the
road' is more difficult than reading the cat sat   on the road. The slower reader has to do more mental work than the faster more smooth reader because he has to add the meaning of each

word to the meaning of each following word. In the above example this amounts to five or six additions. The more efficient reader, absorbing in meaningful units, has only one simple addition.

Another advantage for the faster reader is that his eyes will be doing less physical work on each page. Rather than having as many as 500 fixations tightly focused per page as does the slow reader, he will have as few as 100 fixations per page, each one of which is less muscularly fatiguing.

Yet another advantage is that the rhythm and flow of the faster reader will carry him comfortably through the meaning, whereas the slow reader, because of his stopping and starting, jerky approach, will be far more likely to become bored, to lose concentration, to mentally drift away and to lose the meaning of what he is reading.

It can be seen from this that a number of the commonly held beliefs about faster readers are false:

1 *Words must be read one at a time:* Wrong. Because of our ability to fixate and because we read for meaning rather than for single words.

2 *Reading faster than 500 w.p.m. is impossible:* Wrong. Because the fact that we can take in as many as six words per fixation and the fact that we can make four fixations a second means that speeds of 1,000 are perfectly feasible.

3 *The faster reader is not able to appreciate:* Wrong. Because the faster reader will be understanding more of the meaning of what he reads, will be concentrating on the material more, and will have considerably more time to go back over areas of special interest and importance to him.

4 *Higher speeds give lower concentration:* Wrong. Because the faster we go the more impetus we gather and the more we concentrate.

5 *Average reading speeds are natural and therefore the best:* Wrong. Because average reading speeds are not natural. They are

speeds produced by an incomplete initial training in reading, combined with an inadequate knowledge of how the eye and brain works at the various speeds possible.

Advanced reading techniques

Apart from the general advice given above, some readers may be able to benefit from the following information which is usually practised in conjunction with a qualified instructor:

1 *Visual aid techniques:* When children learn how to read they often point with their finger to the words they are reading. We have traditionally regarded this as a fault and have told them to take their fingers off the page. It is now realised that it is we and not the children who are at fault. Instead of insisting that they remove their fingers we should ask them to move their fingers faster. It is obvious that the hand does not slow down the eye, and the added values that the aid gives in establishing a smooth rhythmical habit are immeasurable.

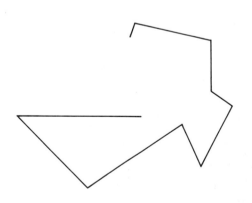

To observe the difference between unaided and aided eye movement, ask a friend to imagine a large circle about one foot in front of him, and then ask him to look slowly and carefully around the circumference. Rather than moving in a perfect circle, his eyes will follow a pattern more resembling an arthritic rectangle. (See fig. 10).

Fig. 10 Pattern showing unaided eye movement attempting to move around the circumference of a circle. See text this page.

Next trace a circle in the air with your finger asking your friend to follow the tip of your finger as you move smoothly around the circumference. You will observe that the eyes will follow almost perfectly and will trace a circle similar to that shown in fig. 11.

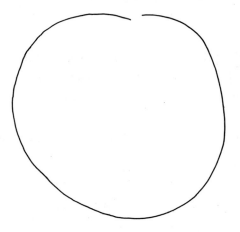

Fig. 11 Pattern showing aided eye movement around the circumference of a circle. See text this page.

This simple experiment also indicates what an enormous improvement in performance there can be if a person is given the basic information about the physical function of the eye and brain. In many instances no long training or arduous practising is necessary. The results, as in this case, are immediate.

The reader is not restricted to the use of his forefinger as a visual aid, and can use to advantage a pen or a pencil, as many naturally efficient readers do. At first the visual aid will make the reading speed look slow. This is because, as mentioned earlier, we all imagine that we read a lot faster than we actually do. But the aided reading speed will actually be faster.

2 *Expanded focus.* In conjunction with visual aid techniques, the reader can practise taking in more than one line at a time. This is certainly not physically impossible and is especially useful on light material or for overviewing and previewing. It will also improve normal reading speeds. It is very important always to use a visual guide during this kind of reading, as without it the eye will tend to wander with comparatively little direction over the page. Various patterns of visual aiding should be experimented with, including diagonal, curving, and straight-down-the-page movements.

3 *High speed perception.* Turning pages as fast as possible attempting to see as many words per page as possible. This form of training will increase the ability to take in large groups of words per fixation, will be applicable to overviewing and previewing techniques, and will condition the mind to much more rapid and efficient general reading practices. This high speed conditioning can be compared to driving along a motorway at 90 miles an hour for one hour. Imagine you had been driving at this speed, and you suddenly came to a road sign saying 'slow to 30'. To what speed would you slow down if somebody covered your speedometer and said 'go on, tell me when you reach 30'. The answer of course would be 50 or 60 m.p.h.

The reason for this is that the mind has become conditioned to a much higher speed, which becomes 'normal'. Previous 'normals' are more or less forgotten in the presence of the new ones. The same applies to reading, and after a high speed practice you will often find yourself reading at twice the speed without even feeling the difference. (See fig. 12).

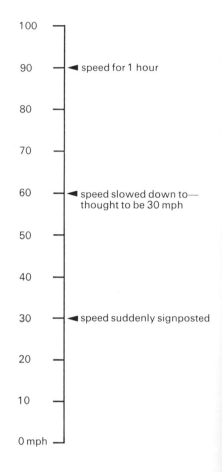

Fig. 12 Illustration showing how the mind 'gets used to' speed and motion. The same kind of relativistic 'misjudgements' can be used to advantage to help us learn to learn more adequately. See text this page.

Motivational practice

Most reading is done at a relaxed and almost lackadaisical pace, a fact which many speed reading courses have taken advantage of. They give their students various exercises and tasks, and suggest to them that after each exercise their speed will increase by 10–20 w.p.m. And so it does, often by as much as 100 per cent over the duration of the lessons. The increase, however, is often due not to the exercises, but to the fact that the student's motivation has been eked out bit by bit during the course.

The same significant increases could be produced by guaranteeing each student, at the beginning of the course, the fulfilment of any wish he desired. Performance would immediately equal those normally achieved at the end of such courses – similar to the unathletic fellow who runs a hundred metres in 10 seconds flat and jumps a 6-foot fence when being chased by a bull. In these cases motivation is the major factor, and the reader will benefit enormously by consciously applying it to each learning experience. If a decision is made to do better, then poor performance will automatically improve.

Metronome training

A metronome, which is usually used for keeping musical rhythm, can be most useful for both reading and high speed reading practices. If you set it at a reasonable pace, each beat can indicate a single sweep for your visual aid. In this way a steady and smooth rhythm can be maintained and the usual slow-down that occurs after a little while can be avoided. Once the most comfortable rhythm has been found, your reading speed can be improved by occasionally adding an extra beat per minute.

The metronome can also be used to pace the high speed perception exercises, starting at slower rates and accelerating to exceptionally fast rates, 'looking' at one page per beat.

The information on eye movements, visual aids and advanced reading techniques should be applied by the reader to each of his reading situations. It will be found that these techniques and items of advice will become more useful when applied together with information and techniques from other chapters, especially the last three dealing with the Organic Study Method.

At the end of this chapter are a series of exercises which give practice in all areas. These exercises should be done in 5 to 20-minute sessions per day, preferably before any normal reading or studying. During the first few weeks as much as half-an-hour per day can be spent profitably. As you become more practised in the exercises they need be done only when revision is felt necessary.

N.B. The formula for working out speed in w.p.m. is:

$$\text{w.p.m. (speed)} = \frac{\text{number of pages read} \times \text{number of words per average page}}{\text{number of minutes spent reading}}$$

EXERCISES

After any w.p.m. calculation enter the number on the graph on page 38.

1 Exercise eye movements over page, moving eyes on horizontal and vertical planes diagonally upper left to lower right, and then upper right to lower left. Speed up gradually day by day. Purpose – to train eyes to function more accurately and independently.

2 Read normally for 5 minutes from a book which you will be able to continue using. Record w.p.m. on continuing graph page 38.

3 Practise turning 100 pages at approximately 2 seconds per page, moving eyes very rapidly down the page. (2 × 2 min. sessions)

Exercises continued

4 a Practise as fast as you can for 1 minute, not worrying about comprehension.
   b Read with motivated comprehension – 1 minute.
   c Calculate and record w.p.m.
Repeat as time allows.

5 Use any book (light material) of your choice, preferably one in which you are interested.
   Try for as much comprehension as possible, but realise that exercise is concerned primarily with speed. In this exercise reading should continue from last point reached.
   a Practise-read for 1 minute at 100 w.p.m. faster than your highest normal speed
   b Practise-read 100 w.p.m. faster than (a).
   c Practise-read 100 w.p.m. faster than (b).
   d Practise-read 100 w.p.m. faster than (c).
   e Practise-read 100 w.p.m. faster than (d).
   f Practise-read with comprehension for 1 minute from point reached at end of (e). Calculate and record w.p.m.

6 High Speed Practice 1
   a Use any easy book. Start from the beginning of a chapter.
   b Practise-read with visual aid, three lines at a time at a *minimum* of 2,000 w.p.m. for 5 minutes.
   c Re-read to mark in 4 minutes.
   d Re-read to mark in 3 minutes.
   e Re-read to mark in 2 minutes.
   f Read on from mark, for same comprehension as at (b) for 5 minutes.

7 High Speed Practice 2
   a Use any easy book, start at the beginning of a chapter.
   b Scan for one minute, using visual aid, 4 seconds per page.
   c Practise-read from the beginning at minimum of 2,000 w.p.m. for 5 minutes.
   d Repeat this exercise when possible.

PROGRESS GRAPH

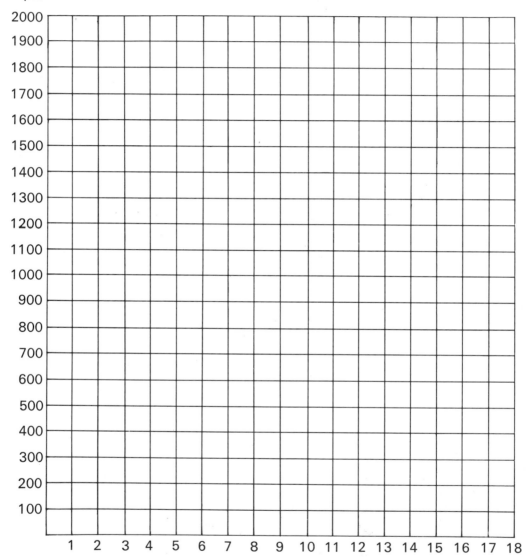

speed wpm

See exercises pages 36/37.

This graph should soon be complete. When it is full make another similar one and keep it in your book.

Personal Notes

Personal Notes

Memory

Overview

- Questions on memory.
- Recall during a learning period.
- Recall after a learning period.
- Review techniques and theory.
- Memory systems – those used by the Greeks and still used by stage performers to astound audiences.
- Key words and concepts for easier methods of using language, noting, learning, thinking and remembering.

Test 1

On the right of these instructions is a list of words. Read each word on this list once, quickly, in order, and then turn to page 46 and fill in as many of the words as you can. You will not be able to remember all of them, so simply try for as many as you can. Read the complete list, one after the other. To ensure you do this properly use a small card, covering each word as you read it.

start now

went
the
book
work
and
good
and
start
of
the
late
white
and
paper
Mohammed Ali
light
of
skill
the
own
stair
note
and
rode
will
time
home

Next turn to page 46, fill in as many of these items as you can, and answer the questions which immediately follow.

Test 2

On page 47 you will find a blank graph. Fill it in with a line which represents the amount you think your memory recalls during a learning period. The vertical left-hand line marks the starting point for the learning; the vertical right-hand line marks the point when learning stops; the bottom line represents no recall at all (complete forgetting); and the top line represents perfect recall.

On the right are examples of graphs filled in by three people.

These graphs start at 75% because it is assumed that most standard learning does not produce 100% understanding or recall.

There are of course many other alternatives, so now turn to page 47 and complete the graph for the way in which you think your recall works.

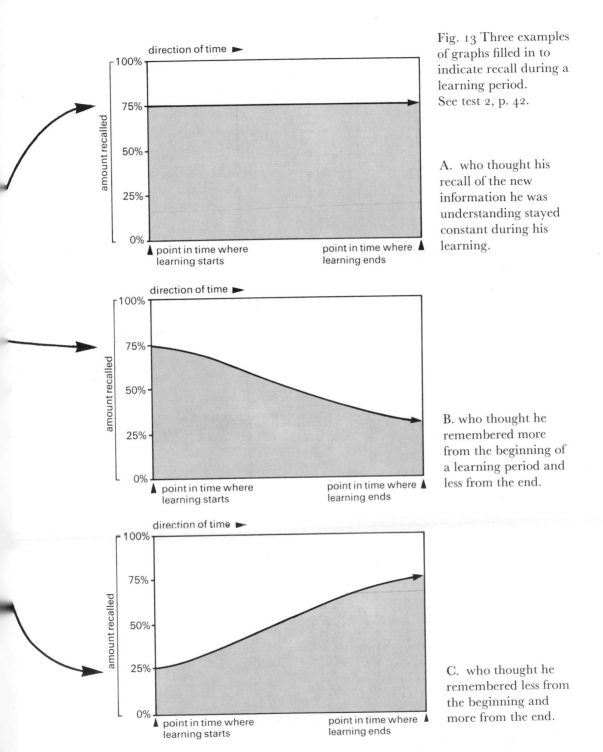

direction of time ▶

amount recalled

100%
75%
50%
25%
0%

▲ point in time where
learning starts

point in time where ▲
learning ends

direction of time ▶

amount recalled

100%
75%
50%
25%
0%

▲ point in time where
learning starts

point in time where ▲
learning ends

direction of time ▶

amount recalled

100%
75%
50%
25%
0%

▲ point in time where
learning starts

point in time where ▲
learning ends

Fig. 13 Three examples
of graphs filled in to
indicate recall during a
learning period.
See test 2, p. 42.

A. who thought his
recall of the new
information he was
understanding stayed
constant during his
learning.

B. who thought he
remembered more
from the beginning of
a learning period and
less from the end.

C. who thought he
remembered less from
the beginning and
more from the end.

Test 3

On page 48 is a blank graph to show the way your memory behaves *after* a learning period has been completed. The vertical left-hand line marks the end point of your learning; there is no right-hand vertical line because it is assumed that the 'afterwards' would be for a few years!; the bottom line represents no recall at all; and the top line represents perfect recall.

The graphs on the right show three people's assessment of their recall after learning.

As with Test 2 there are many alternatives, so now turn to page 48 and complete the graph in the way which most closely represents what you feel to be your normal pattern of forgetting. For the purpose of the exercise you can assume that nothing happens after your learning period to remind you of the information you learned.

Test 4

Here is a list of words next to numbers. As with Test 1 read each item once, covering the ones read with a card as you progress down the list. The purpose of this is to remember which word went with which number:

Now turn to page 48 and fill in the answers in the order requested.

4 glass

9 mash

1 watch

6 chair

10 carpet

5 paper

8 stone

3 orange

7 banana

2 sky

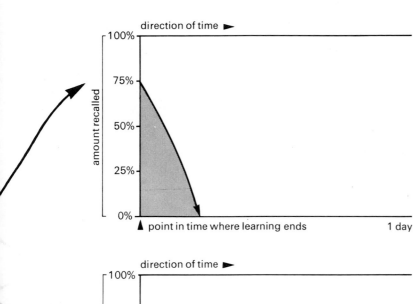

direction of time ▶

100%

75%

50%

amount recalled

25%

0%

▲ point in time where learning ends   1 day

Fig. 14 Three examples of graphs filled in to show recall after a learning period has been completed.
See test 3, p. 44.

A. who thought he forgot nearly everything in a very short period of time.

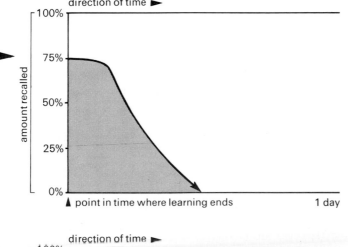

direction of time ▶

100%

75%

50%

amount recalled

25%

0%

▲ point in time where learning ends   1 day

B. who thought his recall was constant for a little while and then dropped off fairly steeply.

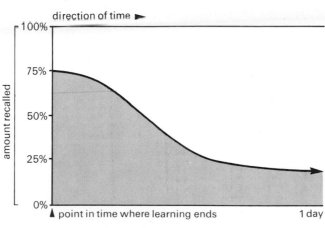

direction of time ▶

100%

75%

50%

amount recalled

25%

0%

▲ point in time where learning ends   1 day

C. who thought his memory stayed constant for a while and then dropped off more slowly, levelling out at a certain point.

Test responses and further questions

Test 1: responses

When answering the questions, do not refer to the original list

1 Fill in as many of the words, in order, as you can.

2 How many of the words from the beginning of the list did you remember before making the first error?

_____

3 Can you recall any words which appeared more than once in the list? If so note them

_____

_____

4 How many of the words within the last five did you remember?

_____

5 Do you remember any item from the list which was outstandingly different from the rest?

_____

6 How many words from the middle of the list can you remember which you have not already noted in answers to previous questions?

_____

_____

_____

_____

Test 2: responses

Fill in, as demonstrated in the examples of fig. 13 page 43, the line which represents the way your memory recalls _during_ a learning period.

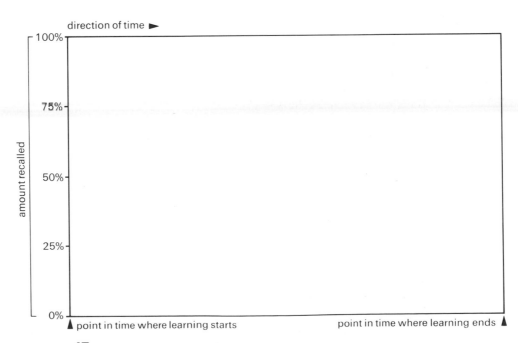

Test 3: responses

Fill in the graph below in the way you think your recall behaves after
a learning period has been completed (see examples fig. 14 page 45).

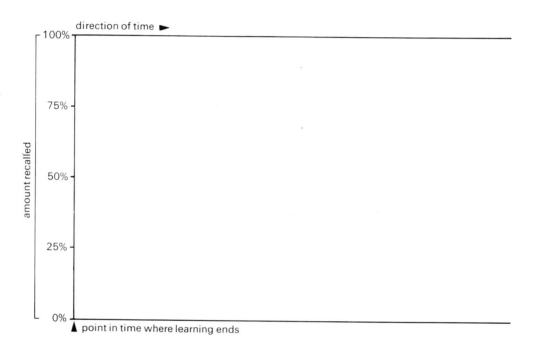

Test 4: responses

Here are the numbers 1 to 10. Fill
in next to each number the word
which originally appeared next to
it. The numbers are not listed in
same order as before. Do not refer
back until you have filled in as
many as you can.

1 _____

7 _____

4 _____

5 _____

6 _____

3 _____

10 _____

8 _____

2 _____

9 _____

Score_____

Recall during learning—discussion of Tests 1 and 2

Test 1 showed how recall functions during a period of learning, as long as understanding remains fairly constant (the words in the list were not 'difficult').

In this test virtually everyone has the following results: anywhere between 2 and 8 of the words at the beginning of the list are recalled; most of the words which appear more than once are recalled (in this case 'the', 'and', 'of'); one or two of the last five words are recalled; and the outstanding word or phrase is recalled (in this case Mohammed Ali); very few of the words from the middle are recalled.

This is a pattern of test scores which shows very dramatically that memory and understanding do not work in exactly the same way as time progresses – all the words were under-

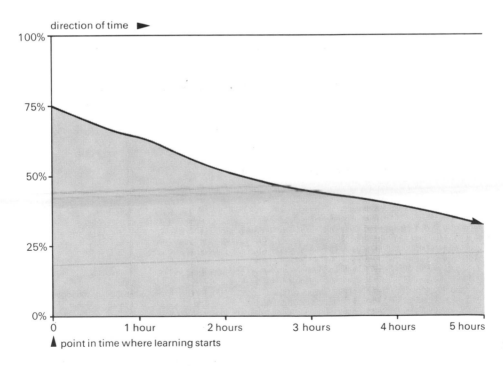

Fig. 15 As time goes on, recall of material being learned tends to get progressively worse unless the mind is given proper rests. See text pp. 49/50.

stood, but only some were recalled. The differences between the way in which memory and understanding function help explain why so many people find they don't recall very much after hours of learning and understanding. The reason is that recall tends to get progressively worse as time goes on unless the mind is given brief rests. (See fig. 15).

Thus the graph requested in Test 2 will be more complex than the simple examples given. It will probably also be more complex than the graph you have traced for your own recall behaviour during learning. Average scores from Test 1 produce a graph similar to fig. 16.

From the graph it is clear that under normal circumstances and with understanding fairly constant, we tend to recall: more at the beginning and ends of learning periods; more of items which are associated by repetition, sense, rhyming etc.; more of things which are outstanding or unique; and considerably *less* of things from the middle of learning periods.

If recall is going to be kept at a reasonable level, it is necessary to find the point at which recall and understanding work in greatest harmony. For normal purposes this point occurs in a time period of between 20 to 40 minutes. A shorter period does not give the mind enough time to appreciate the rhythm and organisation of the material, and a longer period results in the continuing decline of the amount recalled. (As graphed in fig. 17).

If a period of learning from a lecture, a book or the mass media is to take two hours, it is far better to arrange for brief breaks during these two hours. In this way the recall curve can be kept high, and can be prevented from dropping during the later stages of learning. The small breaks will guarantee eight relatively high points of recall, with four small drops in the middle. Each of the drops will be less than the main drop would have been were there no breaks. (See fig. 17).

Breaks are additionally useful as relaxation points. They get rid of the muscular and mental tension which inevitably builds up during periods of concentration.

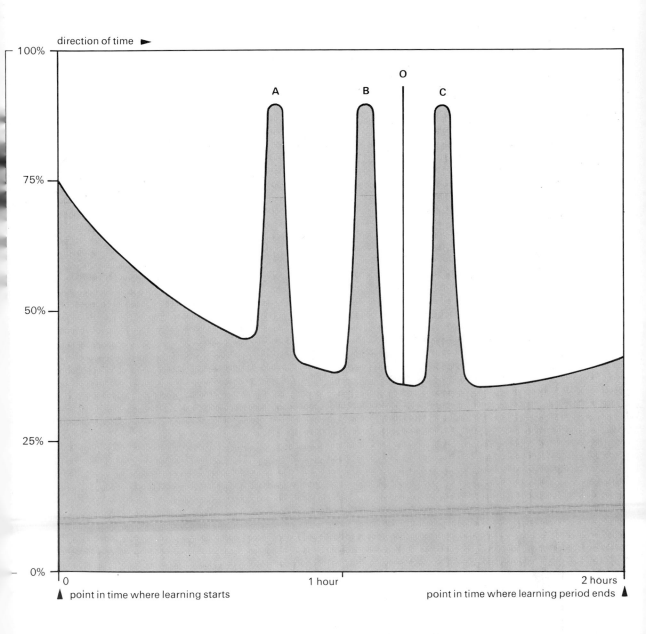

Fig. 16 *Recall during learning – breakdown*
Graph indicating that we recall more from the beginning and ends of
a learning period. We also recall more when things are associated or
linked (A, B and C) and more when things are outstanding or unique
(O). See text pp. 49/50.

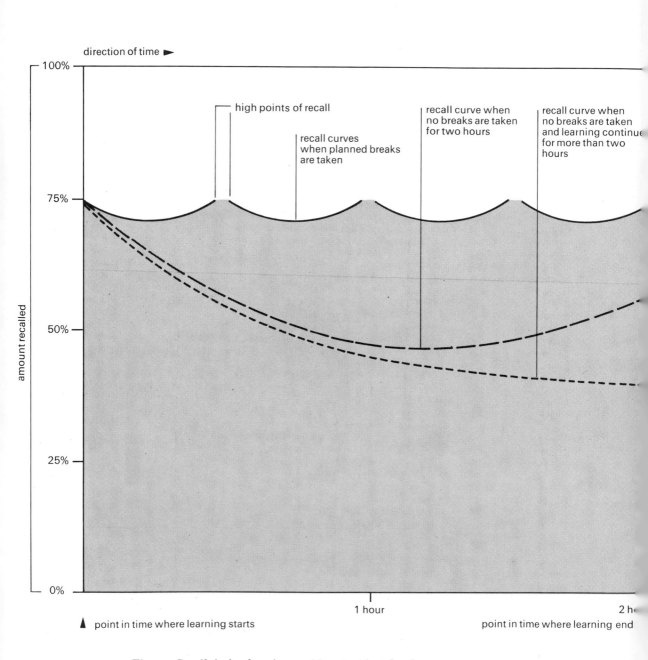

direction of time ▶

100%

high points of recall

recall curve when
no breaks are taken
for two hours

recall curve when
no breaks are taken
and learning continue
for more than two
hours

recall curves
when planned breaks
are taken

75%

amount recalled

50%

25%

0%

1 hour

2 h

▲ point in time where learning starts

point in time where learning end

Fig. 17 *Recall during learning – with and without breaks*
A learning period of between 20–40 minutes produces the best relationship between understanding and recalling. See text pp. 49/50.

Recall after a learning period – discussion of Test 3 and answers

In Test 3 you were asked to fill in a graph indicating the way you thought your recall functioned after a period of learning had been completed. The examples on page 45 were answers many people have given when asked this question, although a much wider variety of responses overall was registered.

Apart from those graphed on page 45 – other answers included: straight lines plunging almost immediately to nothing: variations on the more rapid drop, some falling to 0%, others always maintaining some per cent, however small; variations on the slower fall-off, also with some falling to 0% and others maintaining; and variations on these themes, showing rises and falls of varying degree. (See fig. 18).

The surprising truth of the matter is that none of the examples shown earlier, and none of the estimates shown, are

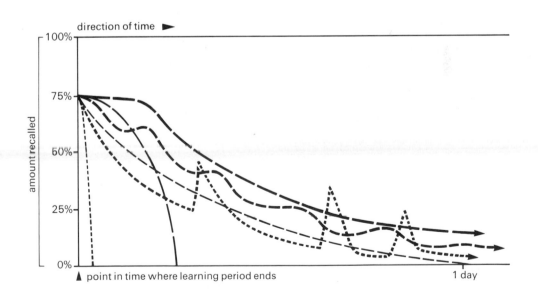

Fig. 18 *Recall after a learning period – people's estimates*
Graph showing the different kinds of answers people gave when asked to show how their recall functioned after a period of learning. See text this page.

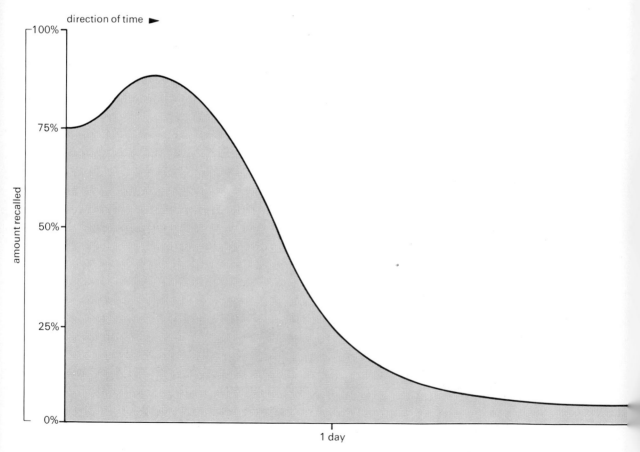

direction of time ▶

amount recalled

100%

75%

50%

25%

0%

1 day

Fig. 19 Graph showing how human recall rises for a short while after learning, and then falls steeply (80% of detail forgotten within 24 hours). See text pp. 54/55.

54

correct. They have all neglected what is perhaps the most important point of all: recall after a learning period initially *rises*, and only then declines, following a steeply falling concave curve that levels off and never quite touches the bottom of the graph. (See fig. 19).

Once it is realised that this brief rise does take place, the reason for it can be understood: at the very moment when a learning period is finished, the mind has had little time to sort out all the new information it has been given, especially the last items. It needs a few minutes to complete and link firmly all the interconnections within the new material.

The decline that takes place after the small rise is a discouragingly steep one – within 24 hours of a one-hour learning period at least 80 per cent of detailed information is lost. This enormous drop in the amount remembered must be prevented, and can be by proper techniques of review.

Memory — review

If review is organised properly, the graph shown in fig. 19 can be changed to keep recall at the high point reached shortly after learning had been completed. In order to accomplish this, a programmed pattern of review must take place, each review being done at the time just before recall is about to drop. For example, the first review should take place about 10 minutes after a one-hour learning period and should itself take 10 minutes. This will keep the recall high for approximately one day, when the next review should take place, this time for a period of 2 to 4 minutes. After this, recall will probably be retained for approximately a week, when another 2 minute review can be completed followed by a further review after about one month. After this time the knowledge will be lodged in Long Term Memory. This means it will be familiar in the way a personal telephone number is familiar, needing only the most occasional nudge to maintain it. (See fig. 20).

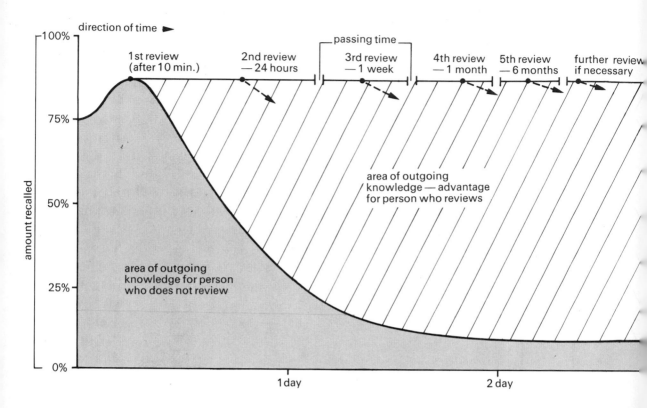

Fig. 20 Graph showing how properly spaced review can keep recall constantly high. See text p. 55.

The first review, especially if notes have been taken, should be a fairly complete note revision which may mean scrapping original notes and substituting for them revised and final copy. The second, third and fourth etc. review sessions should take the following form: without referring to final notes, jot down on a piece of paper everything that can be recalled. This should then be checked against the final notes and any corrections or additions to what has been recalled should be made. Both notes and jottings should be in the form of Recall-

to long term memory

Patterned-Note-Taking as explained on page 104.

One of the most significant aspects of proper review is the accumulative effect it has on all aspects of learning, thinking and remembering. The person who does not review is continually wasting the effort he does put in to any learning task, and putting himself at a serious disadvantage.

Each time he approaches a new learning situation his recall of previous knowledge gained will be at a very low ebb, and the connections which should be made automatically will be missed. This will mean that his understanding of the new material will not be as complete as it could be, and that his efficiency and speed through the new material will also be less. This continuingly negative process results in a downward spiral that ends in a general despair of ever being able to learn anything – each time new material is learned it is forgotten, and each time new material is approached it seems to become more oppressive. The result is that many people, after having finished their formal exams, seldom, if ever, approach text books again.

Failure to review is equally as bad for general memory. If each new piece of information is neglected, it will not remain at a conscious level, and will not be available to form new memory connections. As memory is a process which is based on linking and association, the fewer items there are in the recall store, the less the possibility for new items to be registered and connected.

On the opposite side of this coin, the advantage for the person who *does* review are enormous. The more he maintains his current body of knowledge, the more he will be able to absorb and handle. When he studies, the expanding amount of knowledge at his command will enable him to digest new knowledge far more easily, each new piece of information being absorbed in the context of his existing store of relevant information (see fig. 20). The process is much like that of the traditional snowball rolling, where the snowball gets rapidly bigger the more it rolls and eventually continues rolling under its own momentum.

Digression: review, mental ability and age

The way in which a person reviews has an interesting connection with popular ideas about the way human mental ability declines with age. It is normally assumed that I.Q. scores, recall ability, ability to see spacial relationships, perceptual speed, speed of judgement, induction, figural relations, associative memory, intellectual level, intellectual speed, semantic relations, formal reasoning and general reasoning etc., etc., etc., decline after reaching a peak at the age of 18 to 25 (see fig. 21a). Valid as the figures produced may be, two important factors must be noted:

  1 The decline over the life-time is little more than 5 to 10

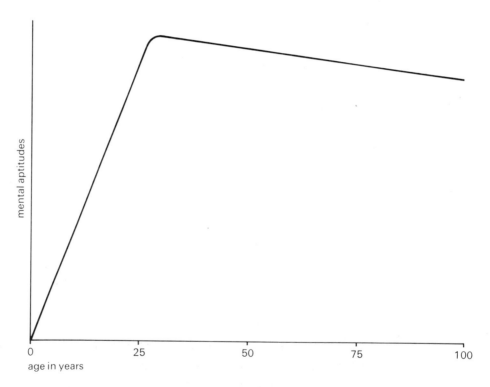

Fig. 21a Graph showing standard results of measuring mental aptitudes as a person gets older. It is assumed that after reaching a peak at approximately 18–25, decline is thereafter slow but steady. See text this page.

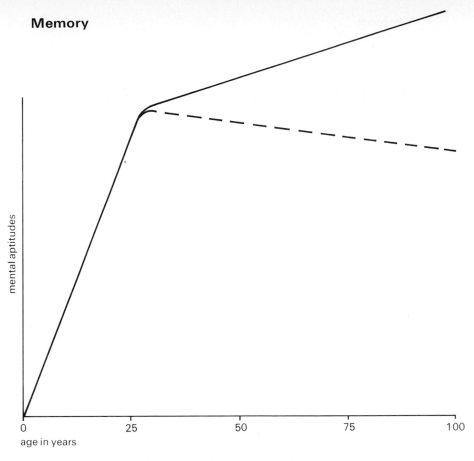

mental aptitudes

0   25   50   75   100

age in years

Fig. 21b Graphs such as shown in fig. 21a are based on statistics from people taught traditionally. A human being would naturally tend to improve these capacities with age if taught properly.

per cent. When considered in relation to the brain's enormous inherent capacity, this is insignificant.

2 The people who took part in the experiments which arrived at these discouraging figures had been educated traditionally, and therefore in most cases would not have been practising proper learning, reviewing and remembering techniques.

Looking at figure 21a it can be easily seen that such a person's mental 'conditioning' would have been at a very low level for an increasing number of years. In other words his real intellectual capacities would have been in 'cold storage'. It is not surprising that such an unused mind would do slightly worse after 20 to 40 years of mis- or no use – it is surprising that it still manages to do as well as it does!

If, on the other hand, the mind were continually used, and its capacities expanded, the effect on the graph for age would be dramatic. This can be seen by taking note of those older people who have remained active and explorative rather than assuming that they were going to get worse as the years passed. Very often their recall is almost total, and their ability to understand and learn new areas of knowledge far surpasses that of equally enthusiastic but younger and less experienced people.

In studying human mental performance it has been mistakenly assumed that the decline found with age is 'natural' and unavoidable. Instead a closer look should be taken at the people being studied, and then experiments should be performed to find out how abilities can be maximised rather than minimised.

Special memory systems—mnemonics (Test 4)

Since the time of the Greeks certain individuals have impressed their fellow men with the most amazing feats of memory. They have been able to remember: hundreds of items backwards and forwards and in any order; dates and numbers; names and faces; and have been able to perform special memory tricks such as memorising whole areas of knowledge perfectly, or remembering decks of cards in the order anyone chose to present them.

In most cases these individuals were using special memorising techniques known as mnemonics. Traditionally these techniques have been scorned as mere tricks, but recently the attitude towards them has begun to change. It has been realised that methods which initially enable minds to remember something more easily and quickly, and then to remember it for much longer afterwards, must be more than simple tricks.

Current knowledge about the ways in which our minds work shows that these techniques are indeed closely connected to the basic ways in which the mind functions. The use of mnemonic techniques has consequently gained respectability and popularity, and they are currently being taught in universities and schools as additional aids in the general learning process. The improvement of memory performances that can be achieved is quite remarkable, and the range of techniques is wide.

There is not enough space in the present chapter to give a complete coverage, but I shall introduce here the basic theory behind the systems, and a simple system for remembering up to ten items.

Let us assume that the items to be remembered are:

1 table
2 feather
3 cat
4 leaf
5 student
6 orange
7 car
8 pencil
9 shirt
10 poker

In order to remember these it is necessary to have some system which enables us to use the associative and linking power of memory to connect them with their proper number.

The best system for this is the Number-Rhyme System, in which each number has a rhyming word connected to it.

The rhyming key words are:

1 bun
2 shoe
3 tree
4 door
5 hive
6 sticks
7 heaven
8 gate
9 vine
10 hen

In order to remember the first list of arbitary words it is necessary to link them in some strong manner with the rhyming words connected to the numbers. If this is done successfully, the answer to a question such as 'what word was connected to number 5?' will be easy: the rhyming word for 5, 'hive', will be recalled automatically and with it will come the connected image of the word that has to be remembered. The numbers, rhyming words, and items to be remembered can be thought of respectively as the clothes rail, the hangers, and the clothes in a clothes cupboard. (See fig. 22).

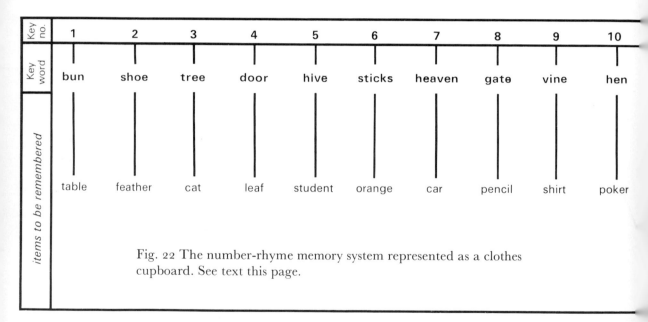

Key no.	1	2	3	4	5	6	7	8	9	10
Key word	bun	shoe	tree	door	hive	sticks	heaven	gate	vine	hen
items to be remembered	table	feather	cat	leaf	student	orange	car	pencil	shirt	poker

Fig. 22 The number-rhyme memory system represented as a clothes cupboard. See text this page.

The important thing in this and all other memory systems is to make sure that the rhyming word and the word to be remembered are totally and securely linked together. In order to do this, the connecting images must be one or many of the following:

exaggerated

The image must be made exceptionally or grotesquely large, or loud, etc.

absurd

Where possible the linked images should form a new image which is humorous or ridiculous.

sexual

If sex can be brought in in anyway, bring it in.

vulgar

Things which are obscene are recalled exceptionally well also!

sensual

As with sex, any of the basic bodily senses will help to form a memorable image.

moving

A moving image usually lasts longer than a static one.

coloured

Coloured as brightly and gaudily as possible.

imaginative

Imaginative in any other way not yet mentioned.

pure

The two items must be linked together with as few other items as possible. Linkages which are too witty, abstract or confused will not help.

It is important, when forming the images, to have a very clear mental picture in front of your inner eye. To achieve this it is often best to close your eyes and to project the image on to the inside of your eyelid.

To make all this clearer, let us try the ten items given.

1 bun   table

Imagine a giant bun on top of a fragile table which is in the process of crumbling from the weight.

2 shoe   feather

Imagine your favourite shoe with an enormous feather growing out of the inside, preventing you from putting your shoe on.

3 tree   cat

Imagine a large tree with either your own cat or a cat you know stuck in the very top branches frantically scrambling about and mewing loudly.

4 door   leaf

Imagine your bedroom door as one giant leaf.

5 hive   student

Imagine a student at his desk, and instead of a book in front of him, imagine an enormous bee hive with bees circling it and occasionally attacking him.

6 sticks   orange

Imagine large sticks puncturing the juicy surface of an orange that is as big as a beach ball.

7 heaven   car

Imagine all the angels sitting on cars rather than clouds.

8 gate   pencil

Imagine a gate made completely out of giant pencils rather than normal wood.

9 vine shirt

Imagine a vine as large as Jack in the Bean Stalk's bean stalk, instead of leaves on the vine hang it all over with brightly coloured shirts blowing in the wind.

10 hen poker

Be vulgar!

Now turn immediately to page 66 and fill in as many of the words as you can.

With a little practice it would be possible to remember ten out of ten each time, even though using the same system. The words to be remembered can, like the clothes they were compared to, be taken off the hook and other clothes substituted. The words which must remain constant and which in any case are almost impossible to forget are the rhyming key words.

As mentioned earlier there are many other systems which are equally as easy to remember as this simple one. Ones which are particularly useful include the Major System, which enables recall of more than a thousand items in the manner of the Number-Rhyme System, as well as giving a key for memorising numbers and dates, and the Face-Name System which helps prevent the embarrassing and wide-spread habit of not being able to recall either the names or faces of people you have met.

Key words and concepts in remembering

As you will have gathered throughout the development of this chapter, memory is primarily an associative and linking process which depends in large part on key words and key concepts properly imagined.

Although the chapter entitled Memory is coming to an end the next three chapters on Key words and Creative pattern linkages are themselves very closely connected with remembering and recalling. The information in this chapter should be reconsidered after the following chapters have been completed.

In the spaces below write the rhyming key word for the Number-Rhyme System, and next to it the words used earlier in the chapter to illustrate the system.

	Rhyming key words	*Word connected*
1		
2		
3		
4		
5		
6		
7		
8		
9		
10		

Personal Notes

Key words – noting

Overview

- Exercise key words; standard responses
- Key words and concepts – creative and recall
- Memory – a comparison between standard note and key word noting
- Transition from advanced key word note taking to advanced creative pattern key word noting

Exercise and discussion

Imagine that your hobby is reading short stories, that you read at least five a day, and that you keep notes so that you will not forget any of them. Imagine also that in order to ensure a proper recall of each story you use a card filing system. For each story you have one card for the title and author, and a card for every paragraph. On each of these paragraph cards you enter a main and a secondary key word or phrase. The key words/phrases you take either directly from the story or make up yourself because they summarise particularly well.

Imagine further that your ten thousandth story is *Kusa-Hibari* by Lafcadio Hearne, and that you have prepared the title-and-author card.

Now read the story on page 69, and for the purpose of this exercise enter a key recall word or phrase for both the main and secondary idea for the first five paragraphs only, in the space provided in table 2, page 72.

Kusa-Hibari

His cage is exactly two Japanese inches high and one inch and a half wide: its tiny wooden door, turning upon a pivot, will scarcely admit the tip of my little finger. But he has plenty of room in that cage-room to walk, and jump, and fly, for he is so small that you must look very carefully through the brown-gauze sides of it in order to catch a glimpse of him. I have always to turn the cage round and round, several times, in a good light, before I can discover his whereabouts, and then I usually find him resting in one of the upper corners – clinging, upside down, to his ceiling of gauze.

Imagine a cricket about the size of an ordinary mosquito – with a pair of antennae much longer than his own body, and so fine that you can distinguish them only against the light. Kusa-Hibari, or 'Grass-Lark' is the Japanese name of him; and he is worth in the market exactly twelve cents: that is to say, very much more than his weight in gold. Twelve cents for such a gnat-like thing! . . . By day he sleeps or meditates, except while occupied with the slice of fresh egg-plant or cucumber which must be poked into his cage every morning . . . to keep him clean and well fed is somewhat troublesome: could you see him, you would think it absurd to take any pains for the sake of a creature so ridiculously small.

But always at sunset the infinitesimal soul of him awakens: then the room begins to fill with a delicate and ghostly music of indescribable sweetness – a thin, silvery rippling and trilling as of tiniest electric bells. As the darkness deepens, the sound becomes sweeter – sometimes swelling till the whole house seems to vibrate with the elfish resonance – sometimes thinning down into the faintest imaginable thread of a voice. But loud or low, it keeps a penetrating quality that is weird . . . . All night the atomy thus sings: he ceases only when the temple bell proclaims the hour of dawn.

Now this tiny song is a song of love – vague love of the unseen

and unknown. It is quite impossible that he should ever have
seen or known, in this present existence of his. Not even his
ancestors, for many generations back, could have known anything of the night-life of the fields, or the amorous value of song.

They were born of eggs hatched in a jar of clay, in the shop
of some insect-merchant: and they dwelt thereafter only in
cages. But he sings the song of his race as it was sung a myriad
years ago, and as faultlessly as if he understood the exact
significant of every note. Of course he did not learn the song.
It is a song of organic memory – deep, dim memory of other
quintillions of lives, when the ghost of him shrilled at night
from the dewy grasses of the hills. Then that song brought him
love – and death. He has forgotten all about death: but he
remembers the love. And therefore he sings now – for the bride
that will never come.

So that his longing is unconsciously retrospective: he cries
to the dust of the past – he calls to the silence and the gods for
the return of time . . . . Human lovers do very much the same
thing without knowing it. They call their illusion an Ideal:
and their Ideal is, after all, a mere shadowing of race-experience,
a phantom of organic memory. The living present has very
little to do with it . . . . Perhaps this atom also has an ideal, or
at least the rudiment of an ideal; but, in any event, the tiny
desire must utter its plaint in vain.

The fault is not altogether mine. I had been warned that if
the creature were mated, he would cease to sing and would
speedily die. But, night after night, the plaintive, sweet, un-
answered trilling touched me like a reproach – became at last
an obsession, an afflication, a torment of conscience; and I
tried to buy a female. It was too late in the season; there were
no more kusa-hibari for sale, – either males or females. The
insect-merchant laughed and said, 'He ought to have died
about the twentieth day of the ninth month.' (It was already
the second day of the tenth month.) But the insect-merchant
did not know that I have a good stove in my study, and keep
the temperature at above 75°F. Wherefore my grass-lark still

sings at the close of the eleventh month, and I hope to keep him alive until the Period of Greatest Cold. However, the rest of his generation are probably dead: neither for love nor money could I now find him a mate. And were I to set him free in order that he might make the search for himself, he could not possibly live through a single night, even if fortunate enough to escape by day the multitude of his natural enemies in the garden – ants, centipedes, and ghastly earth-spiders.

Last evening – the twenty-ninth of the eleventh month – an odd feeling came to me as I sat at my desk: a sense of empti-ness in the room. Then I became aware that my grass-lark was silent, contrary to his wont. I went to the silent cage, and found him lying dead beside a dried-up lump of egg-plant as gray and hard as a stone. Evidently he had not been fed for three or four days; but only the night before his death he had been singing wonderfully – so that I foolishly imagined him to be more than usually contented. My student, Aki, who loves insects, used to feed him; but Aki had gone into the country for a week's holiday, and the duty of caring for the grass-lark had devolved upon Hana, the housemaid. She is not sympathetic, Hana the housemaid. She says that she did not forget the mite – but there was no more egg-plant. And she had never thought of substituting a slice of onion or of cucumber! . . . I spoke words of reproof to Hana the housemaid, and she dutifully expressed contrition. But the fairy-music had stopped; and the stillness reproaches; and the room is cold, in spite of the stove.

Absurd! . . . I have made a good girl unhappy because of an insect half the size of a barley-grain! The quenching of that infinitesimal life troubled me more than I could have believed possible . . . . Of course, the mere habit of thinking about a creature's wants – even the wants of a cricket – may create, by insensible degrees, an imaginative interest, an attachment of which one becomes conscious only when the relation is broken. Besides, I had felt so much, in the hush of the night, the charm of the delicate voice – telling of one minute existence dependent upon my will and selfish pleasure, as upon the favour of a god –

telling me also that the atom of ghost in the tiny cage, and the atom of ghost within myself, were forever but one and the same in the deeps of the Vast of being . . . . And then to think of the little creature hungering and thirsting, night after night and day after day, while the thoughts of his guardian deity were turned to the weaving of dreams! . . . How bravely, nevertheless, he sang on to the very end – an atrocious end, for he had eaten his own legs! . . . May the gods forgive us all – especially Hana the housemaid!

Yet, after all, to devour one's own legs for hunger is not the worst that can happen to a being cursed with the gift of song. There are human crickets who must eat their own hearts in order to sing.

TABLE 2   Key words or phrases for main and secondary ideas from Kusa-Hibari

	main	*secondary*
paragraph 1	————————————	————————————
paragraph 2	————————————	————————————
paragraph 3	————————————	————————————
paragraph 4	————————————	————————————
paragraph 5	————————————	————————————

In table 3 you will find sample key words and phrases from the notes of students who have previously done this exercise. Briefly compare and contrast these with your own ideas.

TABLE 3   Students' suggested key words and phrases

	main	*secondary*
paragraph 1	his cage wooden door ceiling of gauze small insect	two Japanese inches wooden floor plenty of room discover whereabouts
paragraph 2	cricket weight in gold antennae Kusa-Hibari	Grass-Lark twelve cents market gnatlike
paragraph 3	sleep clean and well fed occupied absurd	fresh cucumber pains meditation small
paragraph 4	penetrating music electric bells soul	silvery rippling house vibrating penetrating hour of dawn
paragraph 5	Love amorous the hills Death	night life insect merchant significance love and death

Key words – noting

In the class situation instructors then circled one word from each section:

TABLE 4 *main* *secondary*

paragraph		*main*	*secondary*
	1	wooden door	discover whereabouts
	2	weight in gold	market
	3	occupied	pains
	4	penetrating	hour of dawn
	5	love	night-life

Students were then asked to explain why, in the context of the exercise, these words and phrases and not others had been selected. Answers usually included the following: 'good image words', 'imaginative', 'descriptive', 'appropriate', 'good for remembering', and 'evocative', etc.

Only one student in fifty realised why the instructors had chosen these words: in the context of the exercise the series chosen was disastrous.

To understand why, it is necessary to imagine a time some years after the story has been read when you are going to look at the notes again for recall purposes. Imagine that some friends have played a prank, taking out the title cards of some of your stories and challenging you to remember the titles and authors. You would have no idea to start with to which story your cards referred, and would have to rely solely on them to give you back the correct images.

With the key words from table 4 you would probably be forced to link them in the following way: 'wooden door', a general phrase, would gain a mystery-story air when you read 'discover whereabouts'. The next two keys 'weight in gold' and 'market' would confirm this, adding a further touch of intrigue suggesting a criminal activity. The next three key words, 'occupied' 'pains' and 'penetrating' might lead you to

assume that one of the characters, perhaps the hero, was person-
ally in difficulty, adding further tension to the ongoing plot as
the 'hour of dawn', obviously an important and suspense-filled
moment in the story, approached. The final two keys, 'love'
and 'night-life' would add a romantic or risqué touch to the
whole affair, encouraging you to thumb quickly through the
remaining key words in search of further adventures and
climaxes! You would have created an interesting new story,
but would not remember the original one.

Words which seemed quite good at the time have not, for
some reason, proved adequate for recall. To explain why, it is
necessary to discuss the difference between key recall words
and key creative words, and the way in which they interact
after a period of time has passed.

A key recall word or phrase is one which funnels into itself
a wide range of special images, and which, when it is triggered,
funnels back the same images. It will tend to be a strong noun
or verb, on occasion being surrounded by additional key
adjectives or adverbs. (See fig. 23).

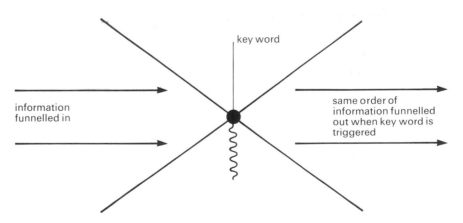

key word

information
funnelled in

same order of
information funnelled
out when key word is
triggered

Fig. 23 Diagram representing key recall word. See text this page.

A key creative word is one which is particularly evocative and image-forming, but which is far more general than the more directed key word. Words like 'ooze' and 'bizarre' are especially evocative but do not bring back a specific image. (See fig. 24)

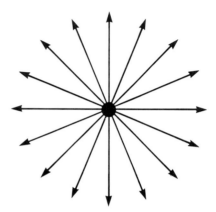

Fig. 24 A key creative word sprays out associations in all directions. See text this page.

Apart from understanding the difference between creative and recall words, it is also necessary to understand the nature of words themselves as well as the nature of the brain which uses them.

Every word is 'multi-ordinate', which simply means that each word is like a little centre on which there are many, many little hooks. Each hook can attach to other words to give both words in the new pair slightly different meanings. For example the word 'run' can be hooked quite differently in 'run like hell' and 'her stocking has a run in it'. (See fig. 25)

In addition to the multi-ordinate nature of words, each brain is also different from each other brain. As shown in the first chapter, the number of connections a brain can make within itself is almost limitless. Each individual also experiences a very different life from each other individual (even if two people are enjoying the 'same experience' together they are in

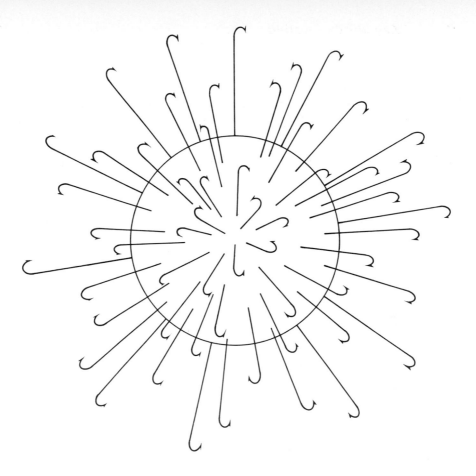

Fig. 25 Each word is multi-ordinate, meaning that it has a large number of 'hooks'. Each hook, when it attaches to another word, changes the meaning of the word. Think, for example, of how the word 'run' changes in different phrase contexts. See text p. 76.

very different worlds: A is enjoying the experience with B as a major part of it, and B is enjoying the experience with A as a major part of it). Similarly the associations that each person will have for any word will be different from everybody else's. Even a simple word like 'leaf' will produce a different series of images for each person who reads or hears it. A person whose favourite colour is green might imagine the general greenness of leaves; someone whose favourite colour is brown, the beauty of autumn; a person who had been injured falling out of a tree, the feeling of fear; a gardener, the different emotions connected with the pleasure of seeing leaves grow and the thought of having to rake them all up when they had fallen, etc. One could go on for ever and still not satisfy the range of associations that you who are reading this book might have when *you* think of leaves.

As well as the unique way in which the mind sees its personal images, each brain is also, by nature, both creative and sense-organising. It will tend to 'tell itself interesting and entertaining stories' as it does for example when we day- or night-dream.

The reason for the failure of the recall and creative words selected from *Kusa-Hibari* can now clearly be seen. When each of the multi-ordinate words or phrases was approached, the mind automatically picked the connecting hooks which were most obvious, most image-producing, or the most sense-making. The mind was consequently led down a path that was more creative than recall based, and a story was constructed that was interesting, but hardly useful for remembering. (See fig. 26).

Fig. 26 Showing how mind can follow the 'wrong connections' in a series of key words. See text this page.

Proper recall words would have forced the mind to make the proper links in the right direction, enabling it to recreate the story even if for all other intentional purposes it had been forgotten. (See fig. 27).

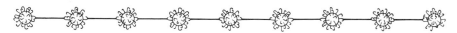

Fig. 27 Direction of correct associations when proper recall key words have been used. See text this page.

Key versus standard notes

The main body of a person's recalling is of this key concept nature. It is not, as is often assumed, a word-for-word verbatim process. When people describe books they have read or places they have been to, they do not start to 're-read' from memory. They give key concept overviews outlining the main characters, settings and events, adding descriptive detail. Similarly the single key word or phrase will bring back whole ranges of experience and sensation. Think for example of the range of images that enter your mind when you read the word 'child'.

How does acceptance of the facts about key recall affect our attitude toward the structure of note taking?

Because we have become so used to speaking and writing words, we have mistakenly assumed that normal sentence structure is the best way to remember verbal images and ideas. Thus the majority of students and even graduates have taken notes in a normal literary fashion similar to the example of a university student whose notes were rated 'good' by his professor. (See page 81).

Our new knowledge of key concepts and recall has shown that in this type of notes 90 per cent of the words are not necessary for recall purposes. This frighteningly high figure becomes even more frightening when a closer look is taken at what happens with standard sentence notes:

1 Time is wasted recording words which have no bearing on memory (estimated waste – 90%).

2 Time is wasted re-reading the same unnecessary words (estimated waste – 90%).

3 Time is wasted searching for the words which *are* key, for they are usually not distinguished by any marks and thus blend in with other non-recall words.

4 The connections between key words are interrupted by words that separate them. We know that memory works by

association and any interference by non recall words will make the connections less strong.

5 The key words are separated in time by intervening words: after one key word or phrase has been read it will take at least a few seconds to get to the next. The longer the time between connections, the less chance there will be of proper connection being made.

6 The key words are separated in space by their distance from each other on the page. As with the point made about time, the greater the distance between the words, the less chance of there being a proper connection.

You are advised to practise key word and phrase selection from any previous notes made during periods of study. It will also be helpful at this point for you to summarise this chapter in key note form.

In addition, reconsider key and creative words in the light of the information in the chapter on Memory, especially the section dealing with mnemonic techniques. Similarly the memory chapter itself can be reconsidered in the light of this chapter, with a similar emphasis on the relationship and similarities between mnemonic systems, key and creative concepts.

The review graph is another important consideration. Review is made much easier when notes are in key form, because less time is expended, and because the recall itself will be superior and more complete. Any weak linkages will also be cemented more firmly in the early stages.

Finally, linkages between key words and concepts should always be emphasised and where possible simple lists and lines of key words should be avoided. In the following chapter advanced methods of key word linking and patterning will be explained in full.

Fig. 28 An example of traditionally 'good' university student's notes. ⟶
See text p. 79.

July 3, 1962. Psychology 205

Books James Coleman Personality Dynamics
       Shaffer, Shoben Psych. of Adjustment.

Course Outline
I Biological Determinants of Behavior the genetic
   approach to behavior v's environmental.
I + II
  II Normal and abnormal behavior.
II Social Determinants of behavior. - class etc.
III Psychological determinants. - approaches to personality
   dynamics ① Psychoanalysis. - Freud, Jung, Adler.
                    "   in therapy.
              ② Perceptual cognitive approach and its
                 approach to psychology and psych. change.

BIOLOGICAL DET'S.
   Heredity produces a given organic structure — it is ∴ imposs.
   to separate genetics from environment in analyzing behav.
   - even growth is not entirely genetic.
   there is no way of saying how much heredity or environment
   affects certain facet of the individual.
* Fuller + Thompson — Behav. Genetics.
   Research Methods for separating environ. from heredity.
   ① Study family lines to look for similarities — family Biography
      - disadv. - may all have had same environment.
   ② Study of Twins — so far the best method
      (a) compare identical twins (monozygotic) vs fraternal
          twins (dizygotic): non-similar heredity.
      (b) co-twin control method - uses only identical twins,
          having one set raised in same home, the other
          set raised apart.
   ③ Hold environ. constant to see what will happen to
      kids of diff. inheritance - Placing kids in foster
      homes, and comparing the diff. in its two homes.

INTELLIGENCE with genet. and environ.
   A. '37 - Newman - compared Binet I.Q. of identical twins in same home,
      with other idet. twins in separate homes. a correlation of
      .67 between reared pairs ∴ genet. influence strong;
      - the corrella. was .91 ∴ diff. was because of environment

Personal Notes

Brain patterns for recall and creative thinking

Overview

- Exercise
- Linear history of speech and print
- Contrast: the structure of the brain
- Advanced note taking and patterning techniques

Exercise

In the space below, and starting immediately after having reached the end of this paragraph, prepare a half-hour speech on the topic of Space Travel. Allow no more than five minutes for the task, whether or not you have finished. This exercise will be referred to later in the chapter, before which time the problems experienced in performing the task should also be noted here.

- Space travel notes

- Problems experienced

Linear history of speech and print

For the last few hundred years it has been popularly thought that man's mind worked in a linear or list-like manner. This belief was held primarily because of the increasing reliance on our two main methods of communication, speech and print.

In speech we are restricted, by the nature of time and space, to speaking and hearing one word at a time. Speech was thus seen as a linear or line-like process between people. (See fig. 29).

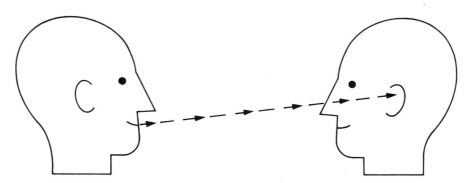

Fig. 29 Speech has traditionally been seen as a list-like affair. See text this page.

Print was seen as even more linear. Not only was the individual forced to take in units of print in consecutive order, but print was laid out on the page in a series of lines or rows.

This linear emphasis overflowed into normal writing or note-taking procedures. Virtually everyone was (and still is) trained in school to take notes in sentences or vertical lists. (Most readers will probably have prepared their half-hour speech in one of these two ways, as shown in fig. 30).

The acceptance of this way of thinking is so long-standing that little has been done to contradict it.

Recent evidence shows the brain to be far more multi-dimensional and pattern making, suggesting that in the speech/print arguments there must be fundamental flaws.

Fig. 30 Standard forms of 'good' or 'neat' notes.

A. Normal line structure – sentenced-based
B. Standard list structure – order-of-importance-based

See text p. 84.

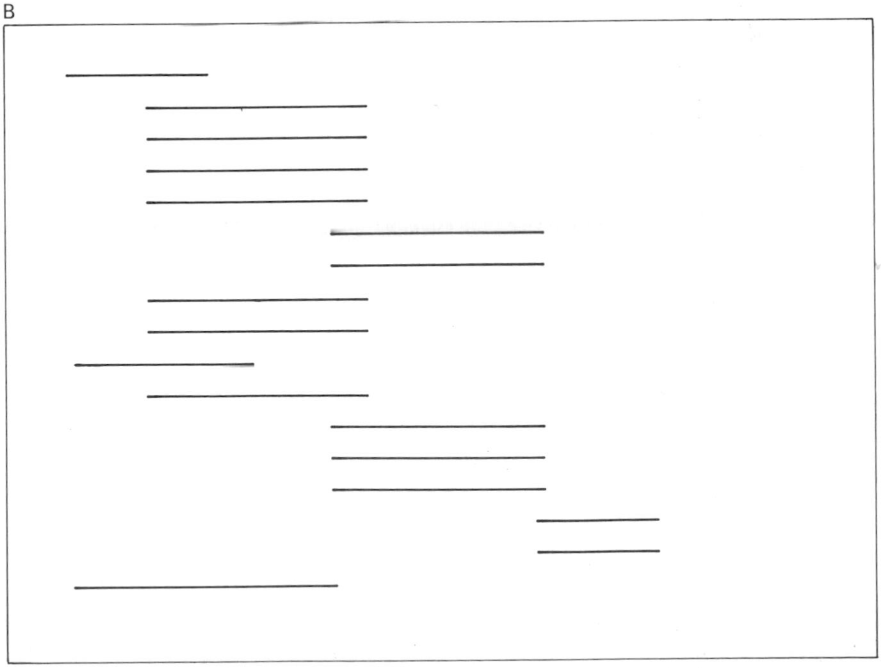

The argument which says that the brain functions linearly because of the speech patterns it has evolved fails to consider, as do the supporters for the absolute nature of I.Q. tests, the nature of the organism. It is easy to point out that when words travel from one person to another they necessarily do so in a line, but this is not really the point. More to the point is, the question: 'How does the brain which is speaking, and the brain which is receiving the words, deal with them *internally*?

The answer is that the brain is most certainly *not* dealing with them in simple lists and lines. You can verify this by thinking of the way in which your own thought processes work while you are speaking to someone else. You will observe that although a single line of words is coming out, a continuing and enormously complex process of sorting and selecting is taking place in your mind throughout the conversation. Whole networks of words and ideas are being juggled and interlinked in order to communicate a certain meaning to the listener.

Similarly the listener is not simply observing a long list of words like someone sucking up spaghetti. He is receiving each word in the context of the words that surround it. At the same time he is also giving the multi-ordinate nature of each word his own special interpretation as dictated by the structure of his personal information patterns and will be analysing, coding and criticising throughout the process. (See fig. 31).

You may have noticed people suddenly reacting to words you liked or thought were harmless. They react this way because the associations they have for these words are different from your own. Knowing this will help you to understand more clearly the nature of conversations, disagreements and misunderstandings.

The argument for print is also weak. Despite the fact that we are trained to read units of information one after each other, that these are presented in lines and that we therefore write and note in lines, such linear presentation is not necessary for understanding, and in many instances is a disadvantage.

The mind is perfectly capable of taking in information which

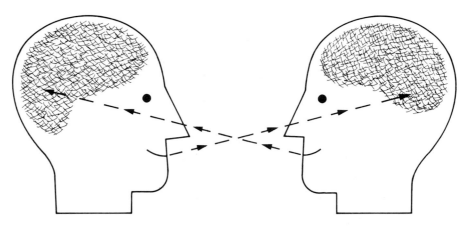

Fig. 31 It is the network inside the mind, and not the simple order of word presentation, which is more important to an understanding of the way we relate to words. See text p. 86.

is non-linear. In its day-to-day life it does this nearly all the time, observing all those things which surround it which include common *non*-linear forms of print: photographs, illustration, diagrams, etc. It is only our society's enormous reliance on linear information which has obscured the issue.

The brain's non-linear character is further confirmed by recent biochemical physiological and psychological research. Each area is discovering that the organism is not only non-linear but is so complex and interlaced as to defy description.

The brain and advanced noting

If the brain is to relate to information most efficiently the information must be structured in such a way as to 'slot in' as easily as possible. It follows that if the brain works primarily

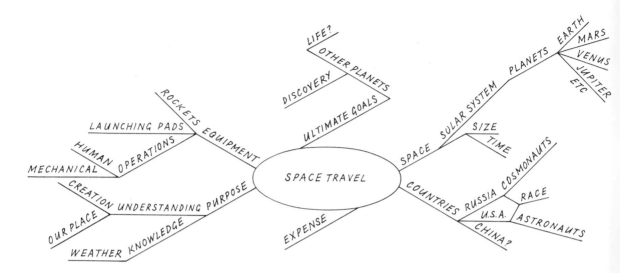

Fig. 32 Initial ideas jotted around a centre. See text pp. 87/8.

with key concepts in an interlinked and integrated manner, our notes and our word relations should in many instances be structured in this way rather than in traditional 'lines'.

Rather than starting from the top and working down in sentences or lists, one should start from the centre or main idea and branch out as dictated by the individual ideas and general form of the central theme. (See fig. 32).

A pattern such as that outlined in fig. 32 has a number of advantages over the linear form of note taking.

1 The centre or main idea is more clearly defined.

2 The relative importance of each idea is clearly indicated. More important ideas will be nearer the centre and less important ideas will be near the edge.

3 The links between the key concepts will be immediately recognizable because of their proximity and connection.

4 As a result of the above, recall and review will be both more effective and more rapid.

5 The nature of the structure allows for the easy addition of new information without messy scratching out or squeezing in, etc.

6 Each pattern made will look and be different from each other pattern. This will aid recall.

7 In the more creative areas of note making such as essay preparations etc., the open-ended nature of the pattern will enable the brain to make new connections far more readily.

In connection with these points, and especially with the last one, you should now do an exercise similar to your space travel speech notes at the beginning of this chapter, but this time using a creative pattern rather than the more linear methods.

In the space provided on page 91 branch out in the manner indicated in figure 32 in preparation for a speech on 'Environmental Problems'. While doing this exercise a number of things should be noted.

1 Words should be printed in capitals. For reading-back purposes a printed pattern gives a more photographic, more immediate, and more comprehensive feed-back. The little extra time that it takes to print is amply made up for in the time saved when reading back.

2 The printed words should be on lines, and each line should be connected to other lines. This is to guarantee that the pattern has basic structure.

3 In creative efforts of this nature the mind should be left as 'free' as possible. Any 'thinking' about where things should go or whether they should be included will simply slow down the process. The idea is to recall everything your mind thinks of around the central idea. As your mind will generate ideas faster than you can write, there should be almost no pause – if you do pause you will probably notice your pen or pencil dithering over the page. The moment you notice this get it back down and carry on. Do not worry about order or organisation as this will in many cases take care of itself. If it does not a final ordering can be completed at the end of the exercise.

Start the exercise now.

Although this first attempt at patterning may have been a little difficult, you will probably have noticed that the experience is quite different from that of the first exercise, and that the problems too may have been quite different.

Problems often noted in the first exercise include;

order	organisation
logical sequence	time distribution
beginning	emphasis of ideas
ending	mental blocking

ENVIRONMENTAL PROBLEMS

These problems arise because people are attempting to select the main headings and ideas one after the other, and are attempting to put them into order as they go – they are trying to order a structure of speech without having considered all the information available. This will inevitably lead to confusion and the problems noted, for new information which turns up after the first few items might suddenly alter the whole outlook on the subject. With a linear approach this type of happening is disruptive, but with the pattern approach it is simply part of the overall process, and can be handled properly.

Another disadvantage of the list-like method is that it operates against the way in which the brain works. Each time an idea is thought of it is put on the list and forgotten while a new idea is searched for. This means that all the multi-ordinate and associative possibilities of each word are cut off and boxed away while the mind wanders around in search of another new idea.

With the pattern approach each idea is left as a totally open possibility, so that the pattern grows organically and increasingly, rather than being stifled.

You might find it interesting to compare your efforts so far with the efforts of three school children. (See figs. 33 to 35).

Figure 33 shows the normal writing of a fourteen-year-old boy who was described as reasonably bright, but messy, confused, and mentally disorganised. The example of his linear writing represents his 'best notes' and explains clearly why he was described as he was. The pattern of English which he completed in five minutes shows almost completely the reverse, suggesting that we can often misjudge a child by the method in which we require him to express himself.

7) SETTING   Time + Places in which the novel is situated

8) IMAGERY   the Kind of images the author uses to describe (usually by simile or metaphor)

9) SYMBOLISM   One thing stands for another
The witches in Macbeth signifying evil

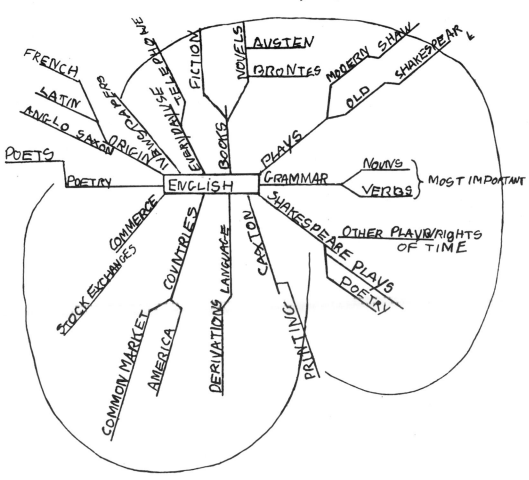

Fig. 33 The 'best notes' in linear writing of a 14 year-old boy, and his pattern notes on English. See text p. 92.

Figure 34 is the pattern of a boy who twice failed O level Economics and who was described by the teacher as having enormous thinking and learning problems combined with an almost total lack of knowledge of his subject. The pattern, which also was completed in five minutes, shows quite the reverse.

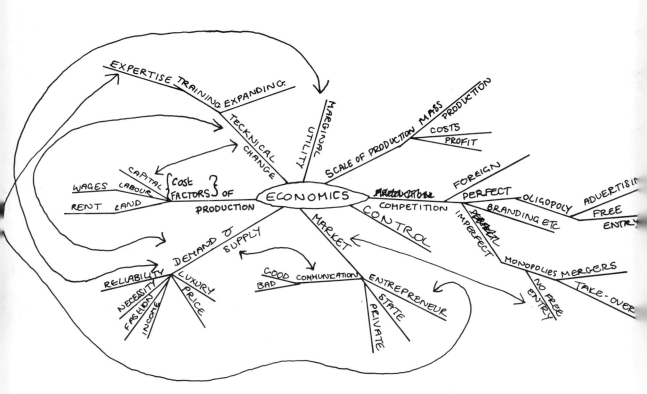

Fig. 34 Pattern by a boy who twice failed O level Economics. See text this page.

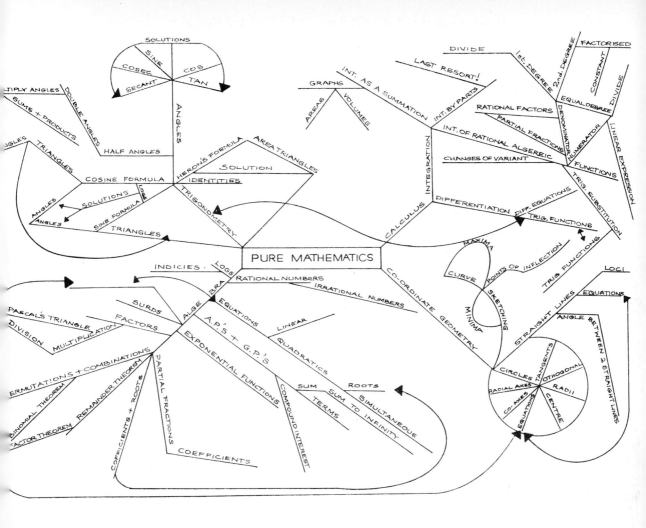

Fig. 35 Pattern by an A level grammar school girl on pure Mathematics. See text this page.

Figure 35 is a pattern done by an A Level grammar school girl on pure Mathematics. When this pattern was shown to a Professor of Mathematics he estimated that it was done by a University Honours student and that it probably took two days to complete. In fact it took the girl only twenty minutes. The pattern enabled her to display an extraordinary creativity in a subject which is normally considered dry, dull and oppressive. Her use of form and shape to augment the words will give an indication of the diversity possible in these structures. The following chapter extends this idea.

Personal Notes

Brain patterns—advanced methods and uses

Overview

- Models for the brain
- Technology and new insights into ourselves
- Advanced brain patterning techniques
- Wider application of patterning techniques

Models of perception—brain—mind

As recently as the 1950s the camera provided the model for our perception and mental imaging: the lens of the camera corresponded to the lens of the eye, and the photographic plate to the brain itself (see fig. 36). This conception was held for some time but was very inadequate. You can confirm this inadequacy

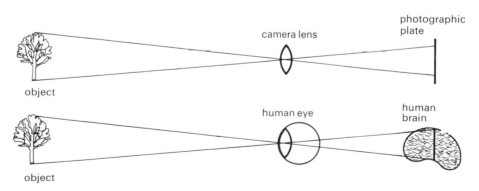

Fig. 36 As recently as 1950 it was thought that the brain operated in ways very similar in part to the camera. See text this page.

by doing the following exercises: in the way that one normally does when drowsily day-dreaming, close your eyes and imagine your favourite object. Having clearly registered the image on your inner eye, perform the following activities.

- Rotate it in front of you
- Look at it from the top
- Look at it from underneath
- Change its colour at least three times
- Move it away as if it were seen from a long distance
- Bring it close again
- Make it gigantic
- Make it tiny
- Totally change the shape of it
- Make it disappear
- Bring it back

These feats can be performed without much difficulty; the apparatus and machinery of a camera could not even begin to perform them.

Modern technology

Recent developments in more refined technology have fortunately given us a much better analogy: the hologram.

In this technique, an especially concentrated light or laser beam is split into two. One half of the ray is directed to the plate, while the other half is bounced off the image and then directed back to the other half of the ray. The special holographic plate records the millions of fragments into which the rays shatter when they collide. (See fig. 37) When this plate is

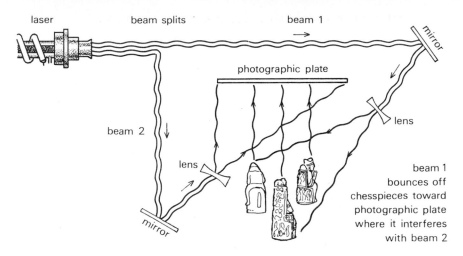

Fig. 37 Diagram showing the use of laser beams in making a holo-gram. See text pp. 98/9.

held up in front of laser beams directed at special angles towards it, the original image is recreated. Amazingly, it is not recreated as a flat picture on the plate, but is perfectly dupli-cated as a three-dimensional ghost object that hangs in space. If the object is looked at from above, below or the side, it is seen in exactly the same way as the original object would be seen. (See fig. 38)

Fig. 38 Two photographs of the same hologram. Each photograph has been taken from a different angle, proving the three-dimensional nature of this new and advanced form of photography. For com-parison of holograms with the brain's function, see text pp. 98/9.

Even more amazingly, if the original holographic plate is rotated through 90 degrees, as many as 90 images can be recorded on the same plate with no interference.

And to add still further to the extraordinary nature of this new development, if the plate is taken and smashed to smithereens with a hammer, each particle of the shattered plate will, when it is placed in front of the specially direct lasers, still produce the complete three-dimensional ghost.

The holograph thus becomes a far more reasonable model than the camera for the way in which our brain works, and begins to give us some idea of just how complex an organism it is that we carry about with us.

But even this extremely refined piece of technology falls far short of the unique capabilities of the brain. The holograph certainly approximates more closely the three-dimensional nature of our imaginations, but its storage capacity is puny compared to the millions of images that our brains can call up at an instant's notice, and randomly. The holograph is also static. It cannot perform any of the directional exercises of the kind described on page 98 which the brain finds so easy and yet which must involve the most unimaginably intricate machinery. And even if the holograph were able to accomplish all this, it would not be able to do what our minds can: to see its own self, with eyes closed, performing the operations!

The above gives considerable cause for thought, and even our most advanced sciences have as yet made little progress in this most interesting area of current research.

Advanced brain-pattern noting

Observing that the brain handles information better if the information is designed to 'slot in', and observing also the information from this chapter about the dimensional nature of the mind, it follows that notes which are themselves more 'holographic' and creative will be far more readily understood, appreciated and recalled. _____

arrows

These can be used to show how concepts which appear on different parts of a pattern are connected. The arrow can be single or multi-headed and can show backward and forward directions.

codes

Asterisks, exclamation marks, crosses and question marks as well as many other indicators can be used next to words to show connections or other 'dimensions'.

geometrical shapes

Squares, oblongs, circles and ellipses etc. . . . can be used to mark areas or words which are similar in nature – for example triangles might be used to show areas of possible solution in a problem-solving pattern. Geometrical shapes can also be used to show order of importance. Some people, for example, prefer to use a square always for their main centre, oblongs for the ideas near the centre, triangles for ideas of next importance, and so on.

artistic three dimension

Each of the geometrical shapes mentioned, and many others, can be given perspective. For example, making a square into a cube. The ideas printed in these shapes will thus 'stand off' the page.

creativity

Creativity can be combined with the use of dimension by making aspects of the pattern fit the topic. One man, for example, when doing a pattern on atomic physics, used the nucleus of an atom and the electrons that surrounded it, as the centre for his pattern.

colour

Colour is particularly useful as a memory and creative aid. It can be used, like arrows, to show how concepts which appear on different parts of the pattern are connected. It can also be used to mark off the boundaries between major areas of a pattern.

There are many devices we can use to make such notes:

Patterns – use

The nature of patterns is intimately connected with the function
of the mind, and they can be used in nearly every
activity where thought, recall, planning or creativity are
involved. Figure 39 is a pattern of the use of patterns,
showing this wide variety of uses. Detailed explanation
of each of these aspects would of course take up a large
book, but in the remainder of this chapter I
shall explain the application of patterns to
the speech writing, essay writing, examination
type of task; to meetings and communications,
and to note taking.

OF MIND FIXATIONS

MENTAL DOODLING

'GETTING OUT

COURSE OUTL

BACKWARD CHILDREN

PARENT/CHILD

TEACHER/CHILD

RELATIONSHIPS

ALL CLASSROOMS

LECTURING

EXPLANATION

Transforming a pattern to a speech, article etc.

Many people, when first shown patterns, assume that they
cannot be used for any linear purpose, such as giving a talk or
writing an article. Nothing could be further from the truth. If
you refer to the pattern of this chapter (between pages 8/9),
you will find how such a transformation took place:

Once the pattern has been completed, the required information is readily available. All that is necessary is to decide the
final order in which to present the information. A good pattern
will offer a number of possibilities. When the choice is being
made, each area of the pattern can be encircled with a different colour, and numbered in the correct order. Putting this
into written or verbal form is simply a matter of outlining the
major areas to be covered, and then going through them point
by point, following the logic of the branched connections. In
this way the problem of redrafting and redrafting yet again is
eliminated – all the gathering and organising will have been
completed at the pattern stage. Using these techniques at
Oxford University, students were able to complete essays in one
third of the previous time while receiving higher marks.

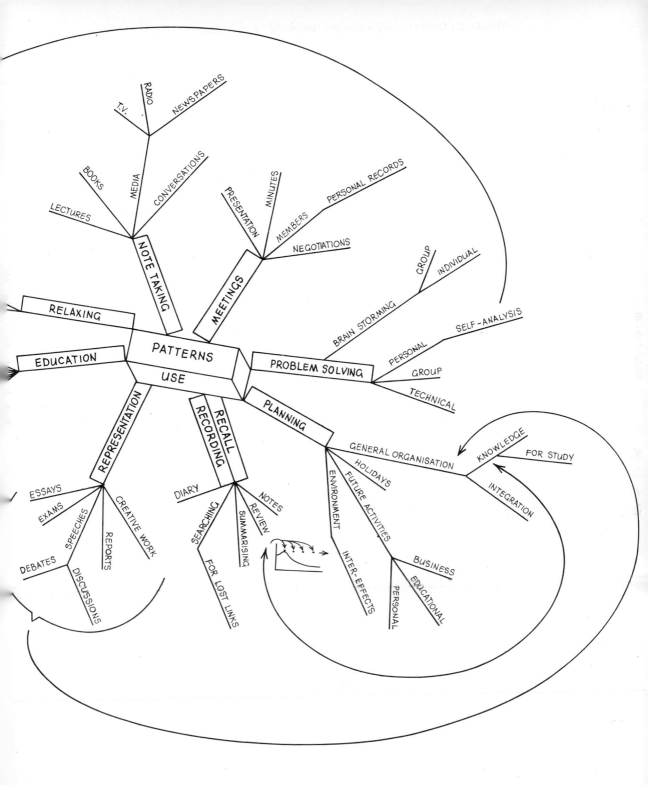

Fig. 39 A pattern on the use of patterns. See text p. 102.

Note taking

It is advisable, when taking notes, to have two blank pages ongoing at the same time. The left-hand page should be for patterned information and the right-hand page for more linear or graphic information such as formulas, special lists, and graphs etc. (See fig. 40).

When taking notes, especially from lectures, it is important to remember that key words and phrases are essentially all that is needed. It is also important to remember that the final structure will not become apparent till the end. Any notes made will therefore probably be semi-final rather than final copy. The first few words noted may be fairly disconnected until the theme of the lecture becomes apparent. It is necessary to understand clearly the value of so-called 'messy' as opposed to 'neat' notes, for many people feel apprehension at having a scrawly, arrowed, non-linear page of notes developing in front of them. 'Neat' notes are traditionally those which are organised in an orderly and linear manner. (See fig. 30 in the previous chapter.) 'Messy' notes are those which are 'untidy' and 'all over the page'. (See fig. 41). The word 'messy' used in this way refers to the *look* and not to the *content*.

In note taking and creative patterning it is primarily the content and not the look that is of importance. The notes which look 'neat' are, in informational terms, messy. As explained on page 92 the key information is disguised, disconnected, and cluttered with many informationally irrelevant words. The notes which look 'messy' are informationally far neater. They show immediately the important concepts, the connections, and even in some cases the crossing-outs and the objections.

Patterned notes in their final form are usually neat in any case and it seldom takes more than ten minutes to finalise an hour's notes on a fresh sheet of paper. This final pattern reconstructing is by no means a waste of time, and if the learning period has been organised properly will fit in perfectly as the first review. (See pages 55/6 and fig. 20).

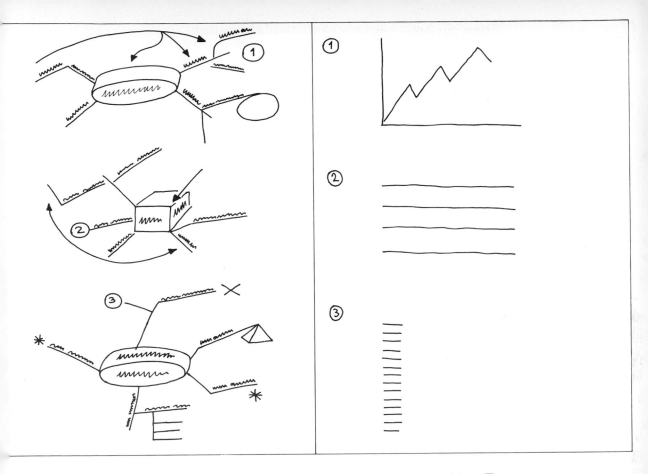

Fig. 40 Showing recommended general form for note taking. Two pages should be used concurrently, one for patterns, the other for graphic or more linear information. These notes may originally 'look messy' but they are in fact neater than traditionally 'neat' notes. See text p. 104.

Communications and meetings

Meetings, notably those for planning or problem solving, often degenerate into situations where each person listens to the others only in order to make his own point as soon as the previous speaker has finished. In such meetings many excellent points are passed over or forgotten, and much time is wasted. A further aggravation is that points which are finally accepted

105

are not necessarily the best, but are those made by the most vociferous or most important speakers.

These problems can be eliminated if the person who organises the meeting uses a creative pattern structure. On a board at the front of the room the central theme of the discussion together with a couple of the sub themes should be presented in basic pattern form. The members of the meeting will have pre-knowledge of what it is about, and will obviously have come prepared. As each member finishes the point he is making, he can be asked to summarise it in key form, and to indicate where on the overall pattern he thinks his point should be entered.

The following are the advantages of this approach:

1 The contribution of each person is registered and recorded properly.
2 No information is lost.
3 The importance given to ideas will pertain more to what was said than to who said it.
4 Digressions and long wafflings will be eliminated because people will be talking more to the point.
5 After the meeting each individual will have a patterned record and will therefore not have lost by the following morning most of what is said.

One further advantage of patterns, especially in note taking and communications, is that the individual is kept continually and actively involved in the complete structure of what is going on, rather than being concerned solely with 'getting down' the last point made. This more complete involvement will lead to a much greater critical and analytical facility, a much greater integration, a much greater ability to recall and a much greater overall understanding.

Personal Notes

The Organic Study Method: Introduction

The subject of Study is divided into three chapters:
Introduction, Preparation, and Application.

Overview

- Problems of 'getting down' to study
- Reasons for the fear and reluctance many people feel when approaching study books
- Problems arising from the use of standard study techniques
- New study techniques

Approaching the study situation – a problem before you start

The Six-O'clock-In-The-Evening-Enthusiastic-Determined-And-Well-Intentioned-Studier-Until-Midnight is a person with whom you are probably already familiar. At 6 o'clock he approaches his desk, and carefully organises everything in preparation for the study period to follow. Having everything in place he next carefully adjusts each item again, giving him time to complete the first excuse: in the morning, he recalls, he did not have quite enough time to read all items of interest in the newspaper. He also realises that if he is going to study it is best to have such small items completely out of the way before settling down to the task at hand.

He therefore leaves his desk, browses through the newspaper and notices as he browses that there are more articles of interest than he had originally thought. He also notices, as he leafs through the pages. the entertainment section. At this point it will seem like a good idea to plan for the evening's first break – perhaps an interesting half-hour programme between 8 and 8.30 p.m.

He finds the programme, and it inevitably starts at about 7 p.m.

At this point, he thinks 'well, I've had a difficult day and it's not too long before the programme starts, and I need a rest anyway, and the relaxation will really help me to get down to studying . . . .' He returns to his desk at 7.45 p.m., because the beginning of the next programme was also a bit more interesting than he thought it would be.

At this stage, he still hovers over his desk tapping his book reassuringly as he remembers that phone call to a friend which, like the articles of interest in the newspapers, is best cleared out of the way before the serious studying begins.

The phone call, of course, is much more interesting and longer than originally planned, but eventually the intrepid studier finds himself back at his desk at about 8.30 p.m.

At this point in the proceedings he actually sits down at the desk, opens the book with a display of physical determination, and starts to read (usually page one) as he experiences the first pangs of hunger and thirst. This is disastrous because he realises that the longer he waits to satisfy the pangs, the worse they will get, and the more interrupted his study concentration will be.

The obvious and only solution is a light snack. This, in its preparation, grows like the associative structure of a creative pattern, as more and more tasty items are linked to the central core of hunger. The snack becomes a feast.

Having removed this final obstacle the desk is returned to with the certain knowledge that this time there is nothing that could possibly interfere with the dedication. The first couple of sentences on page one are looked at again . . . as the studier realises that his stomach is feeling decidedly heavy and a general drowsiness seems to have set in. Far better at this juncture to watch that other interesting half-hour programme at 10 o'clock, after which the digestion will be mostly completed and the rest will enable him to really, *really* get down to the task at hand.

At 12 o'clock we find him asleep in front of the T.V.

Even at this point, when he has been woken up by whoever comes into the room, he will think that things have not gone too badly, for after all he has had a good rest, a good meal, watched some interesting and relaxing programmes, fulfilled his social commitments to his friends, digested the day's information, and got everything completely out of the way so that tomorrow, at 6 o'clock . . . .

The study book is a threat

The above episode is amusing, but the implications of it are significant and serious.

On one level the story is encouraging because, by the very fact that it is a problem experienced by everybody it confirms what has long been suspected: that everyone is basically both creative and inventive, and that the feelings that many have about being uncreative are not necessary. The creativity demonstrated in the example of the reluctant student is not applied very usefully. But the diversity and originality with which we all make up reasons for *not* doing things we should do suggests that each person has a wealth of talent which could be applied in more positive directions.

On another level the story is discouraging because it shows up the wide-spread and underlying fear that most of us experience when confronted with a study text.

This reluctance and fear arises from the examination-based school system in which the child is presented with books on the subjects he is 'taking' at school. He knows that text books are 'harder' than story books and novels; he also knows that they represent a lot of work; and he further knows that he will be tested on his knowledge of the information from the books.

The fact that the type of book is 'hard' is discouraging in itself. The fact that the book represents work is also discouraging, because the child instinctively knows that he is unable to read, note, and remember properly.

But the fact that he is going to be tested is often the most

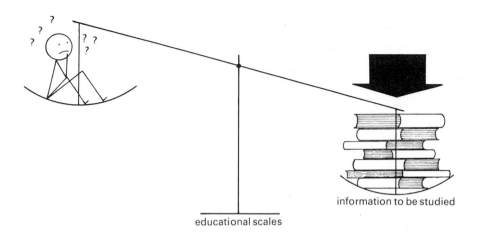

educational scales

information to be studied

Fig. 41 At the present time information is being given more importance and emphasis than the individual. As a result he is being mentally swamped and almost literally 'weighed down' by it all. Both the information and publication explosions are still continuing at staggering rates, while the ability of the individual to handle and study it all remains completely neglected. If he is ever to cope with the situation he must learn not more 'hard facts' but new ways of handling and studying the information – new ways of using his natural abilities to learn, think, recall, create, and solve problems. See also fig. 43 and text p. 115.

serious of the three difficulties. It is well known that this threat can completely disrupt the brain's ability to work in certain situations. The number of cases are enormous of people who literally cannot write anything in an exam situation despite the fact that they know their subject thoroughly – as are the number of cases of people who, even though they are able to write some form of answer, have gigantic mental blocks where whole areas of knowledge are completely forgotten during an exam period. And in even more extreme cases many people have been known to spend a whole two hour period writing frantically, assuming that they were answering the question, but in fact repeating over and over again either their own name or one word.

Faced with this kind of threat, which for many is truly

terrifying, the child has one of two choices: he can either study and face one set of consequences, or not study and face a different set of consequences. If he studies and does badly, then he has proven himself 'incapable', 'unintelligent', 'stupid', a 'dunce' or whatever the appropriate negative expression is at the time. Of course this is not really the case, but he has no way of knowing that in fact it is the system which is not testing him properly.

If he does *not* study, the situation is quite different. Confronted with having failed a test or exam, he can immediately say that of course he failed it because he 'didn't study and wasn't interested in that kind of stuff anyway'.

By doing this, he solves the problem in a number of ways:
1. He avoids both the test and the threat to his self-esteem that studying would involve;
2. He has a perfect excuse for failing;
3. He gets respect from the other children because he is daring to attack a situation which is frightening to them. It is interesting to note that such a child will often find himself in the position of a leader.

It is also interesting to note that even those who do make the decision to study will still reserve a little part of themselves for behaving like the non-studier. The person who gets scores as high as 80 or 90 per cent will also be found using exactly the same excuses for not getting 100 per cent, as the non-studier uses for failing.

Old and new study approaches

The situations described above are unsatisfactory for everyone concerned, and have arisen for various reasons, many of them outlined in earlier parts of this book. One further and major reason for poor study results lies in the way we have approached both study techniques and the information we wanted people to study.

We have surrounded the person with a confusing mass of

different subjects or 'disciplines' demanding that he learn, remember and understand a frightening array under headings such as Mathematics, Physics, Chemistry, Biology, Zoology, Botany, Anatomy, Physiology, Sociology, Psychology, Anthropology, Philosophy, History, Geography, Trigonometry, Paleontology, etc., etc., etc. In each of these subject areas the individual has been and is still presented with series of dates, theories, facts, names, general ideas and so on. (See fig. 42) What this really means is that we have been taking a totally lopsided approach to study and to the way in which a person deals with and relates to the information and knowledge that surrounds him. (See figs. 42 and 43).

As can be seen from the figures we are concentrating far too much on information about the 'separate' areas of knowledge. We are also laying too much stress on asking the individual to feed back facts in pre-digested order or in pre-set forms such as standard examination papers or formal essays.

This approach has also been reflected in the standard study techniques recommended in Schools, Universities, Institutes of Further Education and text books. These techniques have been 'grid' approaches in which it is recommended that a series of steps always be worked through on any book being studied. One common suggestion is that any reasonably difficult study book should always be read through three times in order to ensure a complete understanding. This is obviously a very simple example, but even the many more developed approaches tend to be comparatively rigid and inflexible – simply standard systems to be repeated on each studying occasion.

It is obvious that methods such as these cannot be applied with success to every study book. There is an enormous difference between studying a text on Literary Criticism and studying a text on Higher Mathematics. In order to study properly, a technique is needed which does not force the same approach to such different materials.

First, it is necessary to start working from the individual outwards. Rather than bombarding him with books, formulas

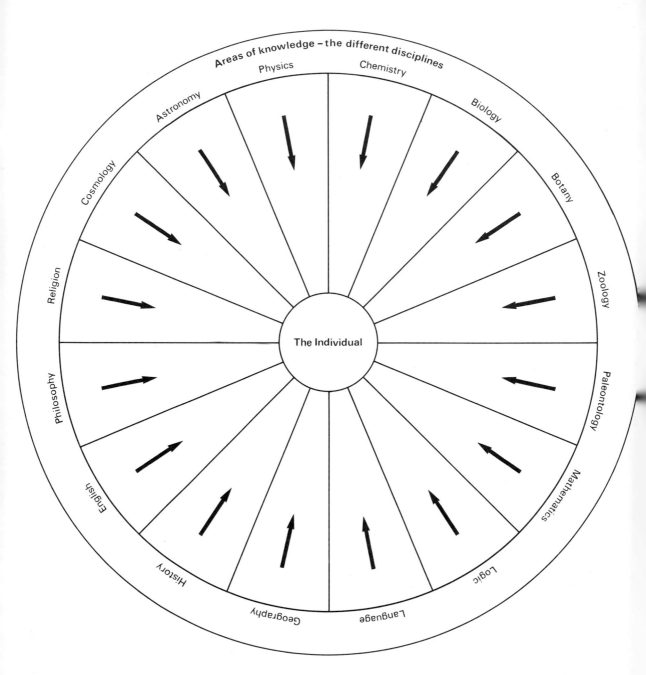

Fig. 42 In traditional education information is given or 'taught' about the different areas of knowledge that surround the individual. The direction and flow is *from* the subject *to* the individual – he is simply given the information, and is expected to absorb, learn and remember as much as he possibly can. See also fig. 41 and text pp. 110/113.

and examinations we must begin to concentrate on teaching each person how he or she *can* study most efficiently. We must teach ourselves how our eyes work when we read, how we remember, how we think, how we can learn more effectively, how we can solve problems and in general how we can best use our abilities, whatever the subject matter.

One is tempted to note here that in our society we have Instruction Manuals and 'How To Do It' booklets on nearly everything, including the simplest of machines. But when it comes to the most complicated, complex, and important organism of all, ourselves, we offer practically no help.

Most of the problems outlined in the first chapter will be eliminated when we finally do change the emphasis away from the subject and information toward the individual and how he can select and understand any information he wants to. People will be equipped to study and remember whatever area of knowledge is interesting or necessary. Things will not have to be 'taught to' or 'crammed in'. Each person will be able to range subjects at his own pace, going for help and personal supervision only when he realises it is necessary. (See fig. 43).

Yet another advantage of this approach is that it will make both teaching and learning much easier, more enjoyable and more productive. By concentrating on the individual and his abilities we will finally and sensibly have placed the learning situation in its proper perspective.

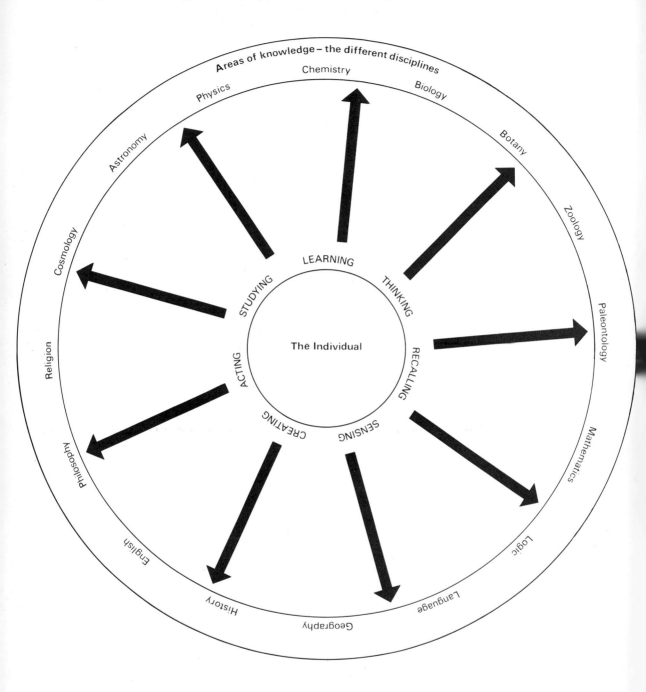

Fig. 43 In the new forms of education, the previous emphases must be reversed. Instead of first teaching the individual facts about other things, we must first teach him facts about himself—facts about how he *can* learn, think, recall, create, and solve problems etc. See text p. 115.

Personal Notes

Personal Notes

The Organic Study Method: Preparation

The Organic Study Method is divided into two main sections: Preparation and Application. Each of these sections is divided into four sub sections:

Preparation	Time
	Amount
	Knowledge
	Questions
Application	Overview
	Preview
	Inview
	Review

It is important to note at the outset that although the main steps are presented in a certain order, this order is by no means essential and can be changed, subtracted from and added to as the study texts warrant.

This chapter will deal with the Preparation section:

Overview

- Deciding on the best use of time
- Defining the areas of study (amount)
- Gathering all the information the reader currently has about the subject
- Defining goals and reasons for studying in the first place

Time and amount

These two aspects can be dealt with together because the theory behind them both is very similar.

The first thing to do when sitting down to study a text book is to decide on the period of time to be devoted to it. Having done this, decide what amount to cover in the time allocated.

119

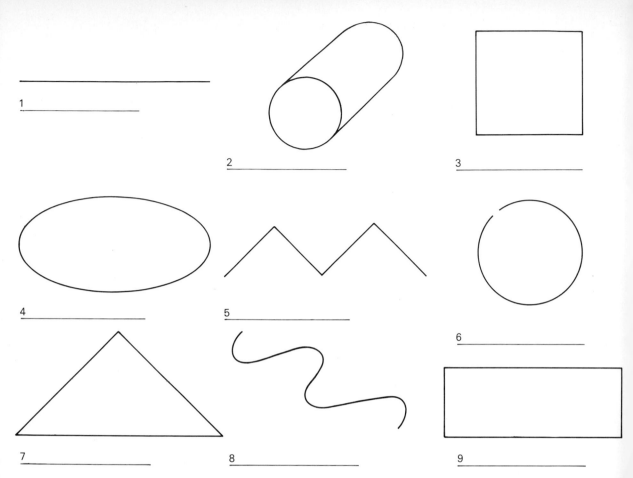

1 _____

2 _____

3 _____

4 _____

5 _____

6 _____

7 _____

8 _____

9 _____

Fig. 44 *Shape recognition*
Enter the name of the shape of each of the items above next to the appropriate number. See text this page *after* completion.

The reason for insisting on these two initial steps is not arbitrary, and is supported by the findings of the Gestalt Psychologists, and some of the most recent findings in Systems Theory (before reading on, look at figure 44).

The Gestalt Psychologists discovered that the human brain has a very strong tendency to complete things – thus most readers will find that they labelled the shapes in figure 44 straight line, cylinder, square, elipse or oval, zig-zag line, circle, triangle, wavy or curved line, rectangle. In fact the 'circle' is not a circle but a 'broken circle.' Many actually see this broken circle as a circle. Others see it as a broken circle but assume that the artist intended to complete it!

120

A more abstract example of our general desire to complete things is our universal tendency as children to build up a language that helps us to make sense of and form completed ideas of our surroundings.

In study, making a decision about Time and Amount gives us immediate knowledge of the entire terrain, as well as the end point or goal. This has the added advantage of enabling the proper linkages to be made rather than encouraging a wandering off in more disconnected ways.

An excellent comparison is that of listening to a lecturer. A good lecturer who is attempting to expound a lot of difficult material will usually explain his starting and his ending points and will often indicate the amount of time he intends to spend on each area of his presentation. The audience will automatically find his lecture easier to follow because they have guide-lines within which to work.

It is advisable to define the amount to be read by placing reasonably large paper markers at the beginnings and ends. This enables the reader to refer back and forward to the information in the amount chosen.

A further advantage of making these decisions at the outset is that the underlying fear of the unknown is avoided. If a large study book is plunged into with no planning, the reader will be continually oppressed by the number of pages he eventually has to complete. Each time he sits down he will be aware that he still has 'a few hundred pages to go' and will be studying with this as a constant and real background threat. If, on the other hand he has selected a reasonable number of pages for the time he is going to study, he will be reading with the knowledge that the task he has set himself is easy and can certainly be completed. The difference in attitude and performance will be marked.

There are still further reasons for making these time and amount decisions which are concerned with the distribution of the reader's effort as time goes on.

Imagine that you have decided to study for two hours and

that the first half-an-hour has been pretty difficult, although you have been making some progress. At this point in time you find that understanding begins to improve and that your progress seems to be getting better and faster.

Would you pat yourself on the back and take a break?

Or would you decide to keep the new and better rhythm going by studying on for a while until you began to lose the new impetus?

Ninty per cent of people asked those questions would carry on. Of those who would take a break, only a few would recommend the same thing to anyone else!

And yet surprisingly the best answer is to take a break. The reason for this can be seen by referring back to the discussion in the chapter on Memory and the amount that is recalled from a period of learning. Despite the fact that understanding may be continually high, the recall of that understanding will be getting worse if the mind is not given a break, thus the graph, fig. 16, is particularly relevant in the study situation. It is essential that any time period for studying be broken down into 20–40 minute sections with small rests in between. (See fig. 17). The common student practice of swotting five hours at a stretch for examination purposes should become a thing of the past, for understanding is *not* the same as remembering, as all too many failed examination papers give witness.

The breaks themselves are also important for a number of reasons.

1 They give the body a physical rest and a chance to relax. This is always useful in a learning situation, and releases the build-up of tension.

2 They enable recall and understanding to 'work together' to the best advantage.

3 They allow a brief period of time for the just-studied information completely to relate each part of itself to the other part, or to intra-integrate. (See fig. 19).

This last point also refers to the Memory chapter and the graph on forgetting as time progresses. During each break the amount of knowledge that can immediately be recalled from the section just studied will increase and will be at a peak as the next section is commenced. This means that not only will more be recalled because the time period itself is best, but also that even more will be recalled because of the rest period.

To assist this even further, do a quick review of what you have read and a preview of what you are about to read at the beginning and end of each study period.

It has taken a number of pages to explain the necessity of deciding on a period of time and on an amount to be covered, but remember that the decisions themselves are extremely brief and will seldom take more than a couple of minutes. When these decisions have been made the next step can be taken:

Noting of knowledge on the subject

Having decided on the amounts to be covered, next jot down as much as you know on the subject as fast as you can. No more than two minutes should be devoted to the exercise. Notes should be in key words and in creative pattern form.

The purpose of this exercise is to improve concentration, to eliminate wandering, and to establish a good mental 'set'. This last term refers to getting the conscious mind filled with important rather than unimportant information. If you have spent two minutes searching your memory banks for pertinent information, you will be far more attuned to the text material, and will be far less likely to continue thinking about the strawberries and cream you are going to have after.

From the time limit of two minutes on this exercise it is obvious that a person's entire knowledge is not required on the pattern – the two minute exercise is intended purely to activate the storage system and to set the mind off in the right direction.

One question which will arise is 'what about the difference if I know almost nothing on the subject or if I know an enormous amount?' If knowledge in the area is great, the two minutes should be spent forming a pattern of the major divisions, theories and names etc. connected with the subject. As the mind can flash through information much faster than the hand can write it, all the minor associations will still be mentally 'seen' and the proper mental set and direction will be established. (See fig. 45).

If the knowledge of the subject is almost nothing, the two minutes should be spent patterning those few items which are known, as well as any other information which seems in any way at all to be connected. This will enable the reader to get as close as he possibly can to the new subject, and will prevent him from feeling totally lost as so many do in this situation. (See fig. 46).

Apart from being immediately useful in study, a continued practice with patterning information gives a number of more general advantages. First, the individual gains by gathering together his immediate and current state of knowledge on areas of his interest. In this way he will be able to keep much more up to date with himself and will actually know what he knows, rather than being in a continually embarrassing position of not knowing what he knows – the 'I've got it on the tip of my tongue', 'if only I could make sense of what I know' pattern of behaviour.

In addition this continued practice of recalling and integrating ideas gives enormous advantage in situations where such abilities are essential: examination, impromptu speeches and answering on the spot questions, to name but a few.

Once the two-minute period is up, the next stage should be moved to immediately.

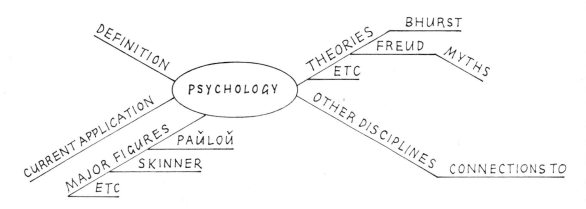

Fig. 45 Knowledge pattern in preparation for study. The studier has some knowledge of the subject before starting. See text p. 124.

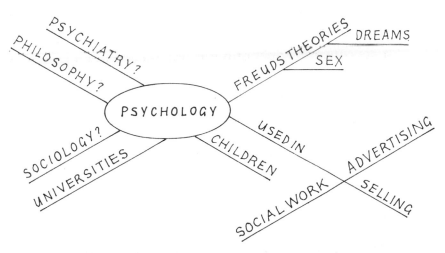

Fig. 46 Knowledge pattern in preparation for study made by a studier with no knowledge of the subject. See text p. 124.

Asking questions—defining goals

Having established the current state of knowledge on the subject, it is next advisable to decide what you want from the book. This involves defining the questions you want answered during the reading. The questions should be asked in the context of goals aimed for and should, like the noting of knowledge, be done in key word and pattern form. Many prefer to use a different coloured pen for this section, and rather than starting a new pattern they add their questions to the already existing pattern on knowledge.

This exercise, again like that for noting knowledge, is based on the principle of establishing proper mental sets. It should also take not much more than two minutes at the outset, as questions can be redefined and added as the reading progresses.

A standard experiment to confirm this approach takes two groups of people who are generally equal in terms of age, education, aptitude etc. Each group is given the same study text and is given enough time to complete either a major section or the whole book.

Group A is told that they are going to be given a completely comprehensive test on everything in the book and that they must study accordingly.

Group B is told that they will be tested on two or three major themes which run through the book, and that they also must study accordingly.

Both groups are in fact tested on the entire text, a situation which one would immediately think unfair to the group that had been told they would be tested only on the main themes.

One might also think that in this situation the second group would do better on questions about the themes they had been given, the first group better on other questions and that both groups might have a similar final score.

To the surprise of many, the second group not only does better on questions about the themes, but they achieve higher total scores which include better marks on all parts of the test.

The reason for this is that the main themes act like great grappling hooks through the information, attaching everything else to them. In other words the main questions and goals acted as associative and linking centres to which all other information became easily attached.

The group instructed to get everything had no centres at all to connect new information to, and because of this were groping through the information with no foundations. It is much like a situation where a person is given so much choice that he ends up making no decision; the paradox where attempting to get everything gains nothing.

Asking questions and establishing goals can be seen, like the section preceding it, to become more and more important as the theory behind becomes better understood. It should be emphasised that the more accurately these questions and goals are established, the more able the reader will be to perform well in the Application section of the Organic Study Method.

Personal Notes

Personal Notes

The Organic Study Method: Application

Overview

- Study Overview
- Preview
- Inview
- Review
  a Memory b Note taking c Visual aiding
  d Continuing review techniques

Study Overview

One of the interesting facts about people using study books
is that most, when given a new text, start reading on page one.
It is *not* advisable to start reading a new study text on the first
page. The following situation is a parallel illustration of this
point:

Imagine that you are a leader of a search party which has
been landed in unknown territory in order to search for a
group of friends who are lost somewhere in the wilderness, and
who have had all radio and other communications cut off.
Upon gathering your forces together you find that all maps,
compasses and other materials for locating yourselves have been
lost. All that is known about the surrounding territory is that
it is very rough terrain, being generally forested, and contain-
ing hills, mountains, swamps, rivers, a few paths and some
slightly more open areas.

In this situation, and assuming that you were still intent on
locating your friends, what would you do to carry out the task
as easily and efficiently as possible?

The inevitable answer, after having rejected such possibilities
as 'give up' and 'hand over command'! is to send out a few

Fig. 47 In the figure above, the patrol group is searching for the lost friends. If it is imagined that the patrol group have just been dropped in the terrain, and have themselves lost all maps and compasses etc., what must their leader first do in order to carry out the mission most effectively and easily? The answer is connected to the reason given for *not* starting to read a study text on the first page (Why not?). See text pp. 130, 132.

131

reconnaissance scouts. Their function being to provide the rescue patrol with all information necessary for overcoming difficulties and finding the most accessible path to your friends.

It should now be clearer why it is not advisable to commence studying on page one, which would be similar to leading all your troops in what seemed to be the best initial direction, with the chance of them all ending up in the swamp.

The difficult study situation can be likened to this example and should be approached similarly: the patrols can be seen as your brain with its varying skills; the lost friends as your studying goals; the mountains and hills as especially difficult areas of text; the swamps as bad literary style; the open spaces as easier passages; and the rivers and paths, as the more direct ways of getting the special information you want.

This illustrates that the most reasonable approach for study texts, especially difficult ones, is to get a good idea of what's in them before charging head-first into a learning catastrophe.

The overview is designed to perform this task. It may be likened to having a helicopter's eye-view of the terrain you are about to cover. It is a reasonably comprehensive covering of the outline of a book. This means that all material not in the regular body of the print should be covered and includes:

back cover	tables	table of contents
marginal notes	illustrations	capitalised words
photographs	subheadings	dates
italics	graphs	footnotes	statistics

The function of this is to provide you with a good knowledge of the graphic sections of the book, not skimming the whole thing, but selecting specific areas for relatively comprehensive coverage. (See fig. 48).

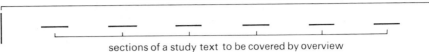

amount of material to be studied

sections of a study text to be covered by overview

Fig. 48 Sections of a study text to be covered by overview. See text p. 132.

It is extremely important to note that throughout the overview a pen, pencil, or other form of visual guide should always be used.

The reason for this can best be explained by reference to a graph. If the eye is unaided, it will simply fixate briefly on general areas of the graph, then move off, leaving only a vague visual memory and an interference to that memory because the eye movement will not have 'registered' the same pattern as the graph.

If a visual aid is used, the eye will more nearly approximate the flow of the graph and the memory will be strengthened by each of the following inputs:

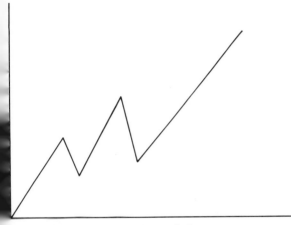

example pattern of graph to be studied

1 The visual memory itself.
2 The remembered eye movement approximating the graph shape.
3 The memory of the movement of the arm or hand in tracing the graph (Kinaesthetic memory).
4 The visual memory of the rhythm and movement of the tracer.

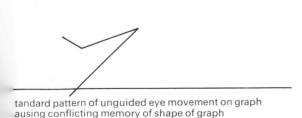

tandard pattern of unguided eye movement on graph ausing conflicting memory of shape of graph

Fig 49

The overall recall resulting from this practice is far superior to that of a person who reads without any visual guide. It is interesting to note that top accountants often use their pens to guide their eyes across and down columns and rows of figures. They do this naturally because any very rigid linear eye movement is difficult to maintain with the unaided eye.

Preview

The second part of study reconnaissance is the preview – covering all that material not covered in the overview. In other words the paragraphed, language content of the book.

During the preview, concentration should be directed to the beginnings and ends of paragraphs, sections, chapters, and even whole texts, because information tends to be concentrated at the beginnings and ends of written material.

If you are studying a short academic paper or a complex study book, the Summary Results and Conclusion sections should always be read first. These sections often include exactly those essences of information that you are searching for, enabling you to grasp that essence without having to wade through a lot of time-wasting material.

Having gained the essence from these sections, simply check that they do indeed summarise the main body of the text.

In the preview, as with the overview, you are not fully reading all the material, but simply concentrating once again on special areas. (See fig. 50)

The value of this section cannot be overemphasised. A case in point is that of a student taught at Oxford who had spent

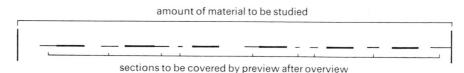

Fig. 50 Sections to be covered by preview after overview. See text this page.

four months struggling through a 500-page tome on psychology. By the time he had reached page 450 he was beginning to despair because the amount of information he was 'holding on to' as he tried to get to the end was becoming too much – he was literally beginning to drown in the information just before reaching his goal.

It transpired that he had been reading straight through the book, and even though he was nearing the end, did not know what the last chapter was about. It was a complete summary of the book! He read the section and estimated that had he done so at the beginning he would have saved himself approximately 70 hours in reading time, 20 hours in note-taking time and a few hundred hours of worrying.

In both the overview and preview you should very actively select and reject. Many people still feel obliged to read everything in a book even though they know it is not necessarily relevant to them. It is far better to treat a book in the way most people treat lecturers. In other words if the man is boring skip what he says, and if he is giving too many examples, is missing the point or is making errors, select, criticise, correct, and disregard as appropriate.

Inview

After the overview and preview, and providing that still more information is required, inview the material. This involves 'filling in' those areas still left. It is *not* necessarily the major reading, as in some cases most of the important material will have been covered in the previous stages. (See fig. 51).

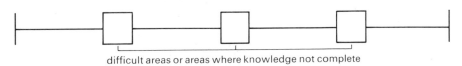

difficult areas or areas where knowledge not complete

Fig. 51 Sections covered after inview has been completed. See text this page.

It should be noted from fig. 51 that there are still certain sections which have been left incomplete even at the inview stage. This is because it is far better to move *over* particularly difficult points than to batter away at them immediately from one side only. They are seldom essential to that which follows them, and the advantages of leaving them are manifold:

1 If they are not immediately struggled with, the brain is given that most important brief period in which it can work on them subconsciously. (Most readers will have experienced the examination question which they 'can't possibly answer' only to find on returning to the question later that the answer pops out and often seems ridiculously simple.)

2 If the difficult areas are returned to later, they can be approached from both sides. Apart from its obvious advantages, considering the difficult area in context also enables the brain's automatic tendency to fill in gaps to work to greater advantage.

3 Moving on from a difficult area releases the tension and mental floundering that often accompanies the traditional approach. (See fig. 52)

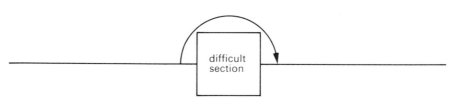

Fig. 52 'Jumping over' a stumbling block usually enables the reader to go back to it later on with more information from 'the other side'. The block itself is seldom essential for the understanding of that which follows it. See text this page.

An adjunct to this last point is that it tends to make studying a more creative process:

Looking at the normal historical development of any discipline, it is found that a fairly regular series of small and logically connected steps are interrupted by great leaps forward.

The propounders of these giant new steps have in many cases 'intuited' them, and afterwards been met with scorn. Galileo and Einstein are examples. As they then explained their ideas step by step, others gradually and progressively understood, some early in the explanation, and others as the innovator neared his conclusion.

In the same manner in which the innovator jumps over an enormous number of sequential steps, and in the same manner in which those who first realised his conclusions did so, the studier who leaves out small sections of study will be giving a greater range to his natural creative and understanding abilities. (See fig. 53)

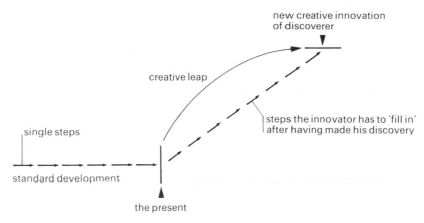

Fig. 53 Historical development of ideas and creative innovations. See text this page.

During the inview initial preparations for note taking should be made. These should include a marking of the previously mentioned difficult areas, as well as areas which the reader considers might be worthy of note.

The marking can be made with a very soft pencil in the margin of the text, and should be in the form of a straight line next to noteworthy material, and a curving line next to material to be reconsidered etc. If the pencil is soft enough, and if a very soft rubber is used, the damage to the book will be less than caused by the average thumb. (See fig. 54).

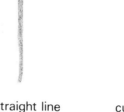

straight line mark for important or noteworthy material

curved line mark for difficult or unclear material

Fig. 54 Marking text

Review

Having completed the overview, preview and inview, and if further information is still required, a review stage is necessary.

In this stage simply fill in all those areas as yet incomplete, and reconsider those sections marked as noteworthy. In most cases it will be found that not much more than 70 per cent of that initially considered relevant will finally be used.

This percentage figure indicates why note taking is left to the last stage: it is difficult to take notes on something one does not know about, and one cannot have knowledge of a section or chapter until it has been completed.

Taking notes at the end of study also avoids those inherent dangers encountered by the person who takes notes as he goes along. For example, you may confront a note from the author explaining that everything up to page 50 in his book can be summarised 'in the following few sentences' after ten or so pages of notes have been taken!

The note taking should be a structure in the form explained on page 104. In study it is especially advisable to keep a large central pattern of the subject area growing in conjunction with the new and smaller patterns from various readings.

This central pattern will obviously be relatively general, but will serve a number of functions:

1 It will give you an immediate, up to date and comprehensive overview of your current knowledge.

2 It will enable you after a reasonable amount of basic study, to see just where the areas of confusion in your subject are, and to see also where your subject connects with other subjects. As such it will place you in the creative situation of of being able to: integrate the known; realise the relevance to other areas; and to make appropriate comment where confusion and debate still exist.

Apart from the immediate review a continuing review programme is essential, and should be constructed in the light of the knowledge we have concerning memory as discussed in the chapter on Memory.

It was seen then that memory did not decline immediately after a learning situation, but actually rose before levelling off and then plummetting. (See fig. 55)

This graph can be warped to your advantage by reviewing just at that point where the memory starts to fall. A review here, at the point of highest memory and integration, will keep the high point up for another one or two days and so on as explained on page 55, see also fig. 56.

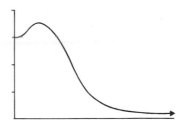

Fig. 55 Graph showing that memory actually rises after learning, before declining sharply.

Fig. 56 This graph shows how quickly forgetting takes place after something has been learned. It also shows how review can 'warp' this graph to enormous advantage. See text this page.

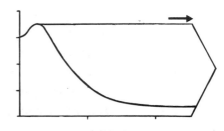

The Organic Study Method: summary

The entire Organic Study Method must be seen not as a step by step progression, but as a series of inter-related aspects of approaching study material. It is quite possible to switch and change the order from the one given here. The amount to be covered may be decided upon before the period of time; the subject matter may be known before the time and amount are decided upon and consequently the knowledge spray pattern could be completed first; the questions can be asked at the preparation stage or after any one of the latter stages; the overview can be eliminated in books where it is inappropriate, or repeated a number of times if the subjects were mathematics or physics. (One student found that it was easier to read four chapters of post-degree mathematics 100 times quickly using the survey technique, than to struggle through one formula at a time. He was of course applying to its extreme, but very effectively, the point made about skipping over difficult areas); a preview can be eliminated or broken down into separate sections; and the inview and review can be variously extended or eliminated.

In other words each subject, and each book of each subject, can be confidently approached in the manner best suited to it. To each book you will bring the knowledge that whatever the difficulties, you possess the fundamental understanding to choose the appropriate and necessarily unique approach.

Study is consequently made a personal, interactive, continually changing and stimulating experience, rather than a rigid, impersonal and tiresomely onerous task.

It should also be noted that despite the apparently greater number of 'times the book is being read', this is *not* the case. By using the Organic Study Method you will be on average reading most sections once only and will then be effectively reviewing those sections considered important. A pictorial representation can be seen in fig. 57.

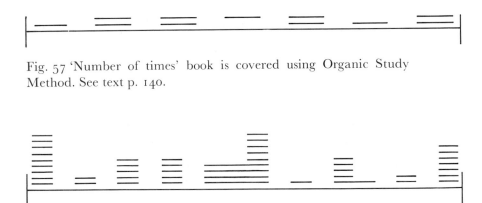

Fig. 57 'Number of times' book is covered using Organic Study Method. See text p. 140.

Fig. 58 'Number of times' book is covered using traditional 'once through' reading techniques. See text pp. 140/1.

By contrast, the 'once through' reader is *not* reading it once through but is reading it an enormous number of times. He thinks he is reading it through once only because he takes in one piece of information after another. He does not realise that his regressions, back-skipping, re-reading of difficult sentences, general disorganisation and forgetting because of inadequate review, result in an actual reading of the book or chapter as many as ten times. (See fig. 58)

As you approach the end of *Use your head* you will be realising that it is not the end, but the real beginning. By now you will have built up a basic structure of the book from which you can construct a pattern of the new information you have acquired. Review this from time to time relating it to aspects of your study and personal life.

Anyone interested in further reading or in courses dealing with the subject covered in *Use your head* can contact the author at 84 Hampstead Way, Hampstead Garden Suburb, London NW11. Tel: 01-455 8266 Telex: 923229.

Personal Notes

Bibliography

Adams, J. A. *Human memory* McGraw-Hill, 1967, o.p.

Alexander, F. M. *Alexander technique: essential writings of F. Matthias Alexander*
ed. E. Maisel. N.J.: Univ. Bks., 1978.

Alexander, F. M. *The resurrection of the body* selected by E. Maisel. New York:
Dell Publishing, paperback 1974.

Alexander, F. M. *The use of the self* Methuen, 1932, o.p.

Bergamini, D. *The universe* Time-Life, 1968.

Bono, E. de *Children solve problems* A. Lane, 1972. o.p.; Penguin Books, 1972. o.p.

Brown, G. S. *Laws of form* Allen and Unwin, 1969. o.p.

Brown, M. E. *Memory matters* David and Charles, 1977.

Buzan, A. *Make the most of your mind* Colt Books, 1977.

Buzan, A. *Speed memory* David and Charles, rev. edn. 1977; Sphere, 1974.

Buzan, A. *Speed reading* David and Charles, rev. edn. 1977; Sphere, 1971

Buzan, A. and Dixon, J. *The evolving brain* David and Charles, 1978.

Cohen, D. *The learning child* Wildwood House, paperback 1973. o.p.

D'Arcy, P. *Reading for meaning* Hutchinson Educational, 2 vols. 1973.

Encyclopaedia Britannica 30 volumes E.B., 1974

Einstein, A. *Relativity* Methuen, 1920 o.p.; University paperbacks rev. edn. 1964, o.p.

Eyken, W. van der *The pre-school years* Penguin Books, n.e. 1977.

Farb, P. *Ecology* Time-Life, 1965.

Freire, P. *Pedagogy of the oppressed* Sheed and Ward, 1972. o.p.; Penguin Books,
1972.

Gattegno, C. *What we owe children* Routledge, 1971; n.e. paperback 1975.

Hall, J. F. *The psychology of learning* Philadelphia; J. B. Lippincott, 1966, o.p.

Harris, E. E. *Hypothesis and perception* Harvester Press, n.e. 1978.

Henry, J. *Essays on education* Penguin Books, 1971. o.p.

Hoggart, R. *The uses of literacy* Chatto and Windus, 1957; Penguin Books, 1969.

Holt, J. *How children fail* Pitman, 1970. o.p.; Penguin Books, 1969.

Huxley, A. *The doors of perception* Chatto, 1968; Panther, 1977.

Illich, I. D. *Deschooling society* Calder and Boyars, 1971; n.e. paperback 1972;
Penguin Books, 1971.

Illich, I. D. *Celebration of awareness* Calder and Boyars, cased and paperback
1971; Penguin Books, 1976.

Julesz, B. *Foundations of Cyclopean perception* Univ. of Chicago Press, 1971.

Klee, P. *Notebooks* vol 1. *The thinking eye* Lund Humphries, 1961.

Lapp, R. E. *Matter* Time-Life, 1965.

Luria, A. R. *The man with a shattered world* Cape, 1973; Penguin Books, 1975. o.p.

McCulloch, W. S. *Embodiments of mind* M.I.T. Press, n.e. paperback 1970.

Maslow, A. H. *Toward a psychology of being* Van Nostrand Reinhold, 2nd edn.
paperback 1969.

Maslow, A. H. *Motivation and personality* Harper and Row, 2nd rev. edn., 1970.

Moore, R. *Evolution* Time-Life, 1969.

Neill, A. S. *Summerhill* Gollancz, 1962; Penguin Books, 1968.

Neumann, J. von *The computer and the brain* Yale University Press, 1958.

Newson, J. and E. *Patterns of infant care in an urban community* Penguin Books, 1965.

Nourse, A. E. *The body* Time-Life, 1966.

Pfeiffer, J. *The cell* Time-Life, 1965.

Postman, N. and Weingartner, C. *Teaching as a subversive activity* Penguin Books, 1971.

Razzell, A. G. *Juniors: postscript to Plowden* Penguin Books, 1968. o.p.

Reimer, E. *School is dead* Penguin Books, 1971.

Rudolph, M. *Light and vision* Time-Life, 1968. o.p.

Saint-Exupery, A. de *The little prince* Heinemann, 1945; Piccolo Books, 1974.

Sandström, C. I. *The psychology of childhood and adolescence* Penguin Books, 1968.

Sawyer, W. W. *Introducing mathematics* vol. 1, *Vision in elementary mathematics* Penguin Books, 1964, o.p.

Schaff, A. *Introduction to semantics* Pergamon Press, 1962. o.p.

Starling, E. H. and Evans, Sir Charles *Principles of human physiology* 14th edn. edited by H. Davson and G. Eggleton. Churchill Livingstone, 1968. o.p.

Suzuki, S. *Nurtured by love* Bosworth Press, 1970.

Tanner, J. M. *Growth* Time-Life, 2nd rev. edn. 1969.

Tolansky, S. *Revolution in optics* Penguin Books, 1968. o.p.

Vaizey, J. *Education for tomorrow* Penguin Books, rev. edn. 1970.

Wilson, J. R. *The mind* Time-Life, 1966.

Wilson, M. *Energy* Time-Life, 1965.

Winnicott, D. W. *The child, the family and the outside world* Penguin Books, 1964.

Yates, F. A. *The art of memory* Routledge 1966; Penguin, rev. edn. 1970.